ULTIMATE GUIDE TO KEYBOARDING

Middle School

by Ask a Tech Teacher©

2023
V2.4

ISBN 978-1-942101-50-5
Printed in the United States of America

Table of Contents

Introduction

Middle School

Table of Figures

Introduction

You may think it impossible to find a keyboarding curriculum that creates accomplished typists from the skimpy amount of time you can devote to keyboarding. You do what you can, but wonder if it's making a difference. Every year, you promise it will go better and then it doesn't. You don't want to give up--research tells us children who learn keyboarding improve academically. It should be an essential skill.

But mid-way through every year, you think of giving up. You have friends who hunt-and-peck as adults and do fine. Does it even matter if students learn to touch type?

Yes, it does.

Don't take my word for it—observe the tech focus by nationally-recognized education standards like Common Core and ISTE.

There is a way to teach keyboarding that works. It requires a plan, faithfully executed, with your eye relentlessly on the goal.

Overview of K-8 Keyboarding

K-1	Introduce mouse skills, key placement, posture
2nd	Work on, key placement, posture, two-hand position
3rd	Reinforce basics. Work on accuracy and technique
4-5	Reinforce basics; continue accuracy, technique. Begin speed
MS	Touch typing

In *The Ultimate Guide to Keyboarding in the Classroom*, we share a curriculum that has succeeded with thousands of students. You'll get directions on what to do, how and when, using mostly free resources.

Big Idea of This Book

Two criteria consistently mentioned in keyboarding research:

1. *Keyboarding instruction is most effective when spread out over several years and designed to build on prior knowledge. (Robinson 1992)*
2. *Once skills are taught, use them, reinforce and refine them (Adams, 1984; Wronkovich, 1998).*

What's that mean? 1) Expect age-appropriate skills, 2) Break practice up into bite-size pieces, 3) Vary lessons, and 4) Infuse keyboarding into all classes.

That's it. We'll show you how.

Overview of the Keyboarding Journey

The overarching objective of keyboarding is to **facilitate communication**. That means 1) students must type fast enough to exceed the speed of their handwriting, and second, they must keep up with their thoughts. Follow this two-book curriculum and the former will occur around fourth grade, the latter in Middle School (Volume II of this curriculum).

Here's an overview of K-MS keyboarding:

K-1	*Introduce mouse skills, keyboarding, key placement, posture*
2nd	*Work on keyboarding, key placement, posture, two-hand position*
3rd	*Reinforce basics. Work on accuracy and technique*
4-5	*Continue accuracy, technique. Begin work on speed*
MS	*Touch typing*

Lessons include lots of variety so you don't get bored. Here's a rundown of activities from kindergarten through eighth grade:

- *digital citizenship*
- *finger exercises*
- *homework (grades 3-8)*
- *keyboarding software*
- *keyboarding websites*
- *problem solving*

- *progress—metric*
- *projects*
- *quiz--blank keyboard (grades 3-8)*
- *shortkeys*
- *students meet grade expectations*

Look for the symbol in each section to see which activities are covered.

Why Learn Keyboarding

If you've ever seen a friend struggle to type a web address or a book report when they don't know where keys are, you know why you want to learn.

Here are more reasons (see Figure 1--some won't apply until college and/or career):

- *to get homework done in a timely manner*
- *to take online quizzes and tests (becoming more common every day)*
- *to complete online classwork—blogs, wikis, websites, discussion boards*
- *to finish timed work before the clock runs out*
- *to talk with friends—email, texting, Twitter, FB (college and career)*
- *to find out more about what interests you (research online)*

- *to do more in the 24 hours of each day*
- *to have more free time for other stuff*
- *when you get a job, they expect you to know keyboarding (college and career)*

Figure 1—How you use keyboarding

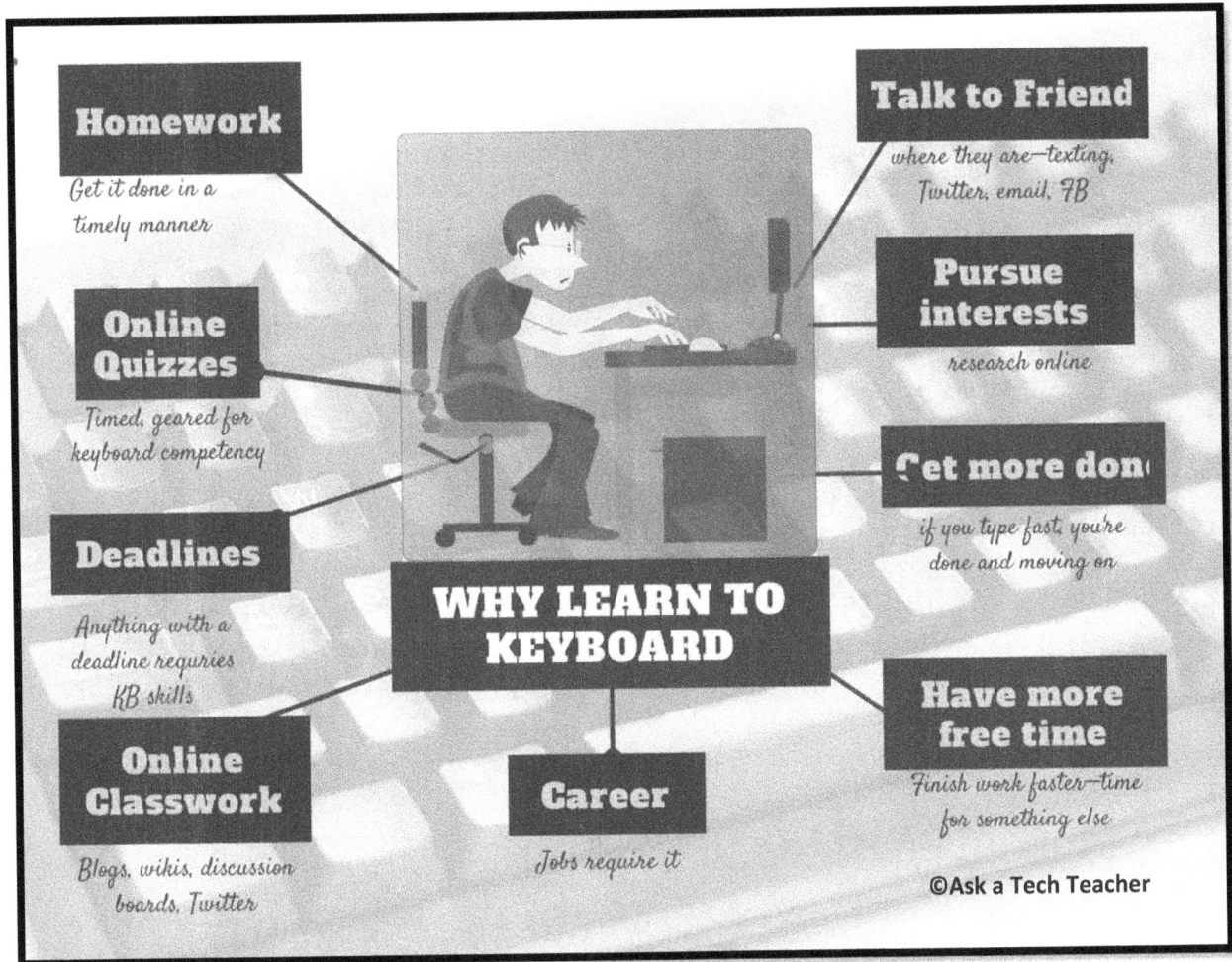

Who Needs This Book

We know you. You are the Tech Specialist, Instructional Technologist, IT Coordinator, Technology Facilitator, Curriculum Specialist, Technology Director, Library Media Specialist—tasked with providing keyboarding skills to meet the challenge of a tech-infused curriculum.

Or you are the school administrator, expected to prepare students for online standardized tests. They practiced last year and it was challenging. You need to fix that.

Just as likely, you are the classroom teacher, a tech enthusiast with a goal to integrate the wonders of technology into lessons. You've seen it work. Others in your PLN do it. And especially now, you want technology to help meet standards like *...use technology strategically and capably... ...use digital resources*. But often, technology seems an add-on to your overflowing educational day.

If you teach in a Common Core state, there are two foundational reasons keyboarding skills are essential:

- Common Core yearly assessments (i.e., PARCC, Smarter Balanced) expect an intermediate knowledge of keyboarding. For example, here's a list of skills collated from PARCC, SPARCC Consortium, and schools taking the test:

  - *Change formatting*
  - *Click/tap*
  - *Constructed response (word limits)*
  - *Copy-paste*
  - *Drag-drop*
  - *Highlight*
  - *Keyboard with sufficient speed and accuracy to complete test on time*
  - *Manipulate graphs*
  - *Use navigation and answer tools*
  - *Plot points*
  - *Run simulations*
  - *Scroll*
  - *Select and drag or slide*
  - *Select area, object, text, multiple items*
  - *Solve tech problems quickly*
  - *Think-while-typing*
  - *Toggle between tabs*
  - *Type on3-three pages at a sitting*
  - *Type with text editor*
  - *Unselect*
  - *Use calculator, protractor, ruler, video*

- Common Core expects the use of technology as a learning tool across all subjects. Keyboarding is fundamental to accomplishing that.

> ***Building student competence and confidence with technology should be part of instruction.***
> ***-- Model Content Frameworks for ELA/Literacy***

To achieve these means students type fast enough to keep up with their thoughts. Follow the lessons in this series and it'll happen.

Common Core Alignment

As you read the Common Core standards, you realize technology is blended throughout as a tool students use to prepare for college and career. For example, read these from Common Core (truncated for easy reading):

- *Expect students to demonstrate sufficient command of **keyboarding** to type a minimum of one page [two by fifth grade, three by sixth] in a single sitting*
- *Expect students to **evaluate different media** (e.g., print or digital ...)*
- *Expect students to **gather relevant information** from print and digital sources*
- *Expect students to integrate and evaluate **information presented in diverse media***
- *Expect students to **interpret information** presented visually, orally, or quantitatively (e.g., ... Web pages)*
- *Expect students make **strategic use of digital media***

> *Use of technology differentiates for student learning styles by providing an alternative method of achieving conceptual understanding, procedural skill and fluency, and applying this knowledge to authentic circumstances*
>
> *--CCSS*

- *Expect students to use **glossaries or dictionaries, both print and digital** ...*
- *Expect students to use information from **illustrations and words in print or digital** text*
- *Expect students to use a **variety of media** in communicating ideas*
- *Expect students to **use technology** and digital media strategically and capably*
- *Expect students to **use text features and search tools** to locate information*

Common Core standards are progressive—students transfer knowledge from one grade to the next where they show evidence of learning by using. Every grade builds on earlier skills to achieve the Standards:

- ***Kindergarten:*** *CCSS.ELA-Literacy.W.K.6 ... explore a variety of digital tools to produce and publish writing, including in collaboration with peers.*
- ***First grade:*** *CCSS.ELA-Literacy.W.1.6 ...use a variety of digital tools to produce and publish writing, including in collaboration with peers.*
- ***Second grade:*** *CCSS.ELA-Literacy.W.2.6 ...use a variety of digital tools to produce and publish writing, including in collaboration with peers.*
- ***Third grade:*** *CCSS.ELA-Literacy.W.3.6 ... use technology to produce and publish writing (using keyboarding skills) as well as to interact and collaborate with others.*
- ***Fourth grade:*** *CCSS.ELA-Literacy.W.4.6 With some guidance and support from adults, use technology, including the Internet, to produce and publish writing*
- ***Fifth grade:*** *CCSS.ELA-Literacy.W.5.6 With some guidance and support from adults, use technology, including the Internet, to produce and publish writing*
- ***Sixth-Eighth grade:*** *CCSS.ELA-Literacy.W.6-8.6 Use tech to produce and publish*

How to Use This Book

This curriculum is part of the K-8 Keyboard system your school has selected to prepare students for keyboarding needs in an education environment. Each lesson is one-two pages (rarely longer) and takes 15 to 30 minutes, with an equal amount of home practice (3rd-8th grade only).

Here's how to decode each lesson (see Figure 2):

Figure 2--Layout of each lesson

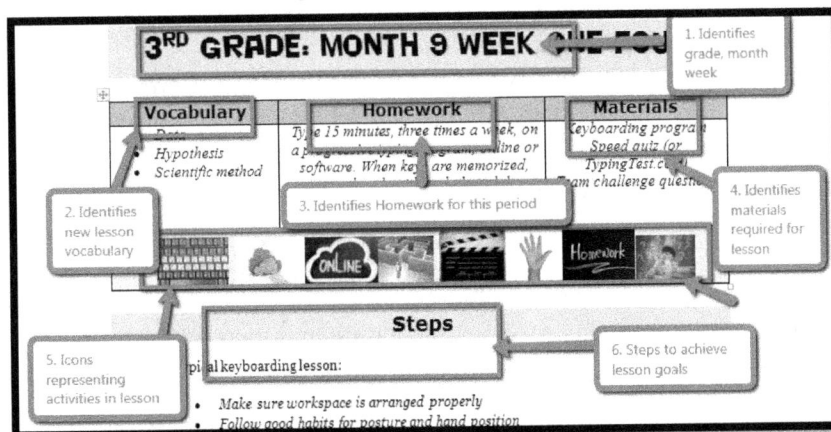

1. ***Grade, month and week—****identifies grade level, month (nine months), week (first three months)*
2. ***Vocabulary—****new domain-specific vocabulary introduced in lesson*

3. ***Homework***—*homework students are expected to complete in the time frame—only applies to grades 3-8. In K-2, this section is for Trouble Shooting*
4. ***Materials***—*identifies what programs, software, web tools, paper items teacher will want prepared for lesson*
5. ***Activities***—*row of icons representing activities included in this lesson. What each icon represents is included under 'Overview of the Keyboarding Journey'*
6. ***Steps***—*steps required for lesson*

Here are tips to get the most out of this curriculum:

- Lessons are device-neutral. It doesn't matter if you're a Mac or PC school or use laptops, desktops, tablets, or Chromebooks. Yes, you might have to make adjustments—but, you're a techie. No worries.
- Topics that relate to keyboarding at all grade levels are included in the beginning portion.
- All teachers share responsibility for student keyboarding. Good keyboarding habits are reinforced by everyone—including parents. Be sure others on the grade-level team understand the elements of keyboarding taught best by project-based learning.
- Every time students use the computer, remind them to set up their workspace correctly and have good posture (see pictures under *Body/Hand Position*).
- Go through lessons in the order presented.
- Several times a month, do finger exercises to remind students that all of their fingers are strong and functional (see detail under *Finger Exercises*).
- Review digital citizenship best practices every time students go online. Make using the internet safely a habit, just as students are careful in their physical neighborhood.
- Expect students to always try to solve techie problems themselves before requesting assistance. The older students are, the more this will happen if you let it. For example, hardware issues (i.e., headphones don't work, monitor doesn't work) can often be solved by kindergarteners once you've provided the tools for analyzing problems.
- Use keyboarding domain-specific vocabulary—especially words in the section, *Vocabulary*, as you teach. There is a lot of vocabulary in the early years and not so much later.
- Lessons use free software and web-based tools where possible. If you can't access one, email info@structuredlearning.net and a curriculum specialist will help you develop a work-around.
- Because each monthly and weekly group of activities may take place over multiple time periods, lessons include an underscore (_____) in front of parts. Check off (in the manner allowed by your digital reader) what you complete and proceed from there next time.
- As students finish each activity and/or skill, check it off on ***Ready to Move On*** at the month-end and the checklist at year-end. Don't go to a new month or year until all is completed.
- At every opportunity, use keyboarding in class projects. These will be assessed by class teacher.

> *Students advancing through the grades are expected to meet each year's grade-specific standards, retain or further develop skills and understandings mastered in preceding grades...*
>
> *--from Common Core*

> *Building student competence and confidence with technology should be part of instruction.*
>
> *-- Model Content Framework for ELA/Literacy*

- Students work at their own pace. They aren't pressured to keep up or forced to slow down. If they finish the year early, offer alternatives (fun keyboarding sites, do homework during keyboarding time, play Minecraft—you pick).
- You'll find a lot of links in this ebook, but know this: **Links die.** If a link doesn't work, try a different one (usually there are options) or contact Zeke.Rowe@StructuredLearning.net. He'll help.
- Every effort has been made to provide a written-out link to online resources for those using the print book. If you come across a link that you can't access, here's what to do:

  - *Google the name. Some of them will pop up right away*
  - *See if we've provided the link in another part of the book*
  - *Contact Zeke at Structured Learning--*zeke.rowe@structuredlearning.net*. You can even do this first. He'll find it—no worries.*

- Assessments include (see ***Assessments*** for detail):

  - Daily/weekly: Homework
  - Once each grading period: speed/accuracy quiz (grades 3-8)
  - Once each grading period: blank keyboard quizzes (grades 3-8)
  - End of year: Team Challenge—work with a group to see who knows the most, the fastest
  - Self-evaluation on a shared class spreadsheet, affirming completion of tasks. Provide a link (to shared Google spreadsheet or similar) to update.
  - Formative assessments during classtime

- When assessments are successfully passed, award the Certificate found under *Templates*.
- Encourage students (when age-appropriate for your student group) to set up **backchannel communication,** especially for Middle Schoolers since much of their keyboard learning is done outside the class. Encourage them to share lessons, ideas, and more.
- If you would like these lessons blended into an overarching K-8 tech curriculum, as part of a larger goal of teaching students technology skills, check out the K-8 technology curriculum (http://www.structuredlearning.net/book/k-8-tech-curriculum-set/).
- *If you're using the K-8 student eworkbooks, have one available each lesson so you see what students are reading. If you don't have them—that's fine. They are similar to any subject workbook--these lessons through the eyes of the student.*

Equipment Needs

This curriculum is platform-neutral and device-agnostic. It doesn't matter if you have PCs or Macs (or a Linux hybrid). It doesn't matter if they run off of desktops or laptops or netbooks or Chromebooks.

No iPads, though, unless they have attached keyboards.

What goes well with this curriculum?

- This keyboarding curriculum has **two volumes**—one for Lower grades (Elementary) and one for Middle School. If you don't have both and want them, check Structured Learning.net.
- **Grades K-8 student eworkbooks**—require nominal guidance from teacher using this two-volume keyboard curriculum. Students use workbook materials to proceed at their own pace for the entire school year. Each is 70-90 pages, digital delivery. Free with class set of eworkbooks: this

Ultimate Guide to Keyboarding and grades 3-8 student companion videos. *Note: If you purchased class-set of workbooks, we'll credit this teacher manual.*

- **Grades 3-8 student companion videos**—for students using the workbooks. Twelve videos, 1-2 per month, to support student learning through the eworkbooks. *Note: if you own a class-set of student eworkbooks, companion videos are free. If you purchased the videos first and then decided to add the class-set of student workbooks, we'll credit the price of the videos.*
- **Classroom posters**—decorate your classroom with keyboarding reminders.
- **Articles on keyboarding pedagogy**—most popular articles from *Ask a Tech Teacher* on keyboarding, how-tos and pedagogy.
- **K-8** tech skills curriculum—integrates keyboarding into a larger goal of learning tech skills.
- **K-5** tech curriculum companion wikis—while these focus on all tech skills, each lesson (32 per year per grade level) includes keyboarding. About 10-15 minutes. *Note: Free if you own the K-8 tech skills curriculum*
- **Summer immersion**—an intensive fifteen-day course of keyboarding done online over the summer. An hour a day, five days a week, three weeks. Fifteen videos. Great way for students to kick-start their next year keyboarding needs

How to Contact us

Email for purchase questions: zeke.rowe@structuredlearning.net
Email for curriculum questions: askatechteacher@gmail.com
Twitter: @askatechteacher

License

If you purchased this ebook, you have a single-user license. You are welcome to make copies of **individual pages.** To reproduce the **entire book** for a class, multiple teachers, school, or district, please contact the publisher for a multi-user license.

Assessments

A complete list of yearly assessments, alphabetized

Blank Keyboard Quizzes

Grades 3-8, taken once a grading period. They focus on key placement. Students get five-fifteen minutes to fill in blank keys, depending upon grade level and your unique group. Here's a sample of important keys:

Figure 3--Important keys

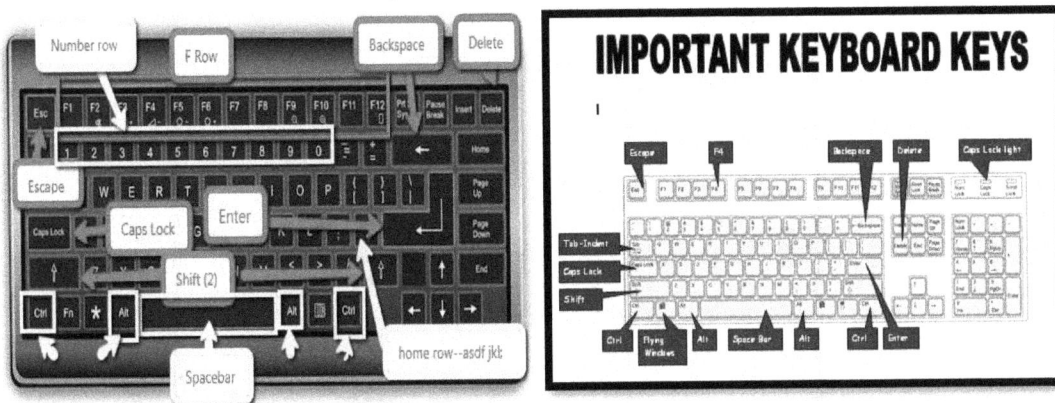

Here's a sample of the two blank keyboard quizzes:

Figure 4--Blank keyboards (2)

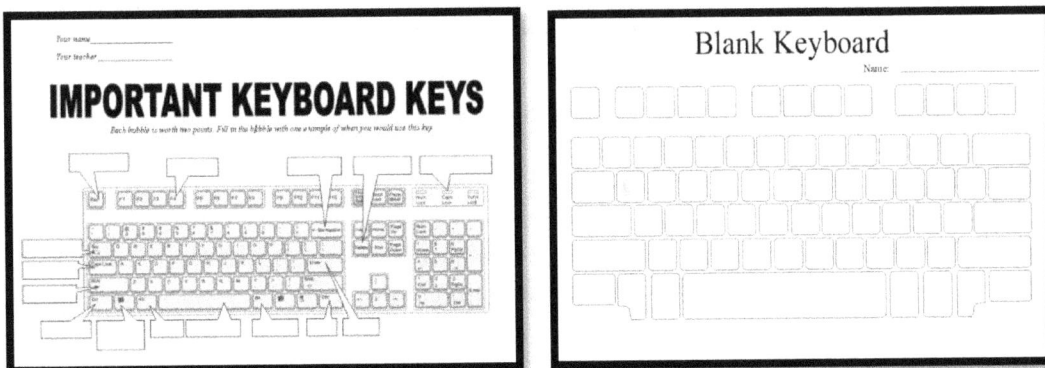

See full-size examples in *'Templates'*.

Formative

Grades K-8: As students practice during class, walk around and observe. Don't assess right/wrong, rather progress, ability to adopt proper form, attention to work, and higher-order thinking skills.

Hardware

Grades 2-5: These are parts of the computer system students should be familiar with. This assessment is taken early in the year for olders and late in the year for youngers. They are the first pieces students will be able to troubleshoot as they keyboard.

Only use this in Middle School if students are unfamiliar with it:

Figure 5--Parts of the computer

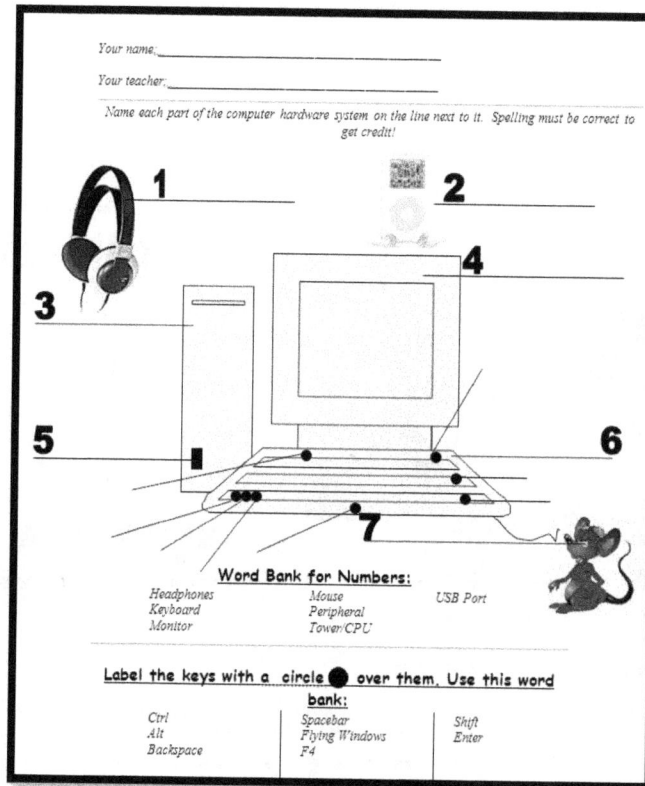

See *Templates* for a blank you can use to test student knowledge.

Homework

Grades 3-8: Students are assigned keyboarding homework that triples the time they spend practicing keyboarding. For example, if they work on keyboarding 15 minutes a week at school, expect 30-60 minutes at home (less for youngers, more for olders).

There are lots of options for grading homework. Here are a few:

- *Student emails teacher 1) that s/he finished, 2) how s/he used keyboarding in other classes, 3) how keyboarding homework made typing in other classes easier*
- *Autonomous assessment, the assumption being if students don't do homework, they won't do well on periodic quizzes*
- *Students who don't improve on quizzes are required to attend after-school practice sessions. They retake the assessment to 'pass out' of class*

- *Parents confirm student completion of homework by filling out a monthly checklist. No submittal, no credit. See Figure 6 for an example:*

Figure 6--Keyboard homework verification

TECHNOLOGY CLASS

Keyboard Homework

Student_____ Teacher_____

Month_____

Parents: Please fill in the sites your child visited (TTL4, Dancemat Typing, Typing Web) and how long they practiced (expectation is ten minutes a week). Be sure to sign each entry.

Turn the completed form into Lab 105

Week	Site	Minutes	Parent Signature
1.			
2.			
3.			
4.			

Ultimately, you decide what works for your students. You want it rigorous without being onerous.

Self-assessment

Grades 5-8: A collaborative spreadsheet updated weekly/monthly by students and shared with you. This begins when you decide your unique group should start. Here's an example in Google Apps:

Figure 7--Keyboard homework--self-assessment

	A	B	C	D	E	F	G	H	I	J	K	L	M	N	O	P	Q	R	S	T	U	V
1							KEYBOARDING MONTH															
2			Set-up				Month 1						Month 2						Month 3			
3		set up wiki pg	set up blog	dig note-tkg	Poll	ET	WPM	HW	TT	BKA	ET	NT	WPM	HW	TT	BKA	ET	NT	WPM	HW	TT	BKA
4	AISHA																					
5	ALOMNA																					
6	ANDY																					
7	CHIP																					
8	DAVIS																					
9	DELBERT																					
10	GEORGE																					
11	JASON																					
12	JO-ANNY																					
13	JUSTIN																					
14	JUTE																					
15	LAD																					
16	LEO																					
17	LUIZ																					
18	LUJA																					
19	MACIAS																					
20	MORRIS																					
21	PAULO																					
22	PETER																					

Speed/accuracy Quiz

Grades 3-8: Taken each grading period. The first is a benchmark, the student's starting point. Everyone gets 100%. Each after is graded based on improvement as follows:

- *20% improvement   10/10*
- *10-20% improvement   9/10*

- *1-10% improvement*   8/10
- *No improvement*   7/10
- *Slowed down*   6/10

Grade level standards are (adjust for your unique student group):

6th Grade:	*35wpm*
7th Grade:	*40 wpm*
8th Grade:	*45 wpm*

Team Challenge

Grades 4-8: Last class of the year, students participate in a keyboarding Team Challenge. Prior to its start: Students work with classmates to develop a list of questions they think address growth in keyboarding skills. This includes posture, keyboarding tips, key positions, purpose of non-letter keys, which finger to use for what.

Students study the questions before the Challenge—in teams—and strategize for the best way to win.

The Team Challenge takes about thirty minutes. During the Challenge, the moderator asks a question from the list and each team gets three seconds to answer—no thinking! They can answer verbally or with the correct finger. Why so quick? Because keyboarding requires finding keys automatically, without thinking.

Figure 8 is a thumbnail—full size sample is under 'Templates':

Figure 8--Team Challenge--keyboarding

ANNUAL TEAM CHALLENGE—KEYBOARD

Review

Review the following concepts. These are similar to questions that will be asked during the upcoming Team Challenge to find the summer's most tech-savvy student!

1. What's the computer log in
2. What's the computer password
3. What's your password for TTL4
4. What row do your finger start on before you even type a letter
5. What's the row above home row
6. What's the row below home row called
7. How do you find the f and j key without looking
8. Name three keys you use your pinkie to push
9. Name three keys you use your ring finger to push
10. Name three keys you use your middle finger to push
11. Name three keys you use your pointer to push
12. Name one key you use your right thumb to push
13. Which finger do you use for the backspace key
14. Which finger do you use for the shift key
15. Which finger do you use for the enter key
16. Which finger do you use for the escape key
17. What are three rules of how you sit at the keyboard
18. Do you have cat's paws or dog paws at the computer
19. Why (do you use cat's paws or dog paws)
20. What part of the chair do you sit on when keyboarding
21. Where are your elbows when keyboarding
22. Where does your right thumb rest when keyboarding
23. What is typing without looking at the keys called
24. Which finger pushes the a key
25. Which finger pushes the b key
26. Which finger pushes the ac key
27. Which finger pushes the d key
28. Which finger pushes the e key
29. Which finger pushes the f key
30. Which finger pushes the g key
31. Which finger pushes the h key
32. Which finger pushes the i key
33. Which finger pushes the j key
34. Which finger pushes the k key
35. What finger pushes enter
36. What's the keyboard shortcut to exit a program
37. As a general rule, which finger pushes a key
38. How do you capitalize a letter
39. As a general rule, do you fingers move or your hands in finding the keys
40. What is one keyboard shortcut
41. What is a desktop

Research

If you're like many teachers I've talked to, you ask yourself (or parents in your school ask) the following questions before committing the time necessary for a comprehensive keyboarding program:

1. *Can elementary school children learn to keyboard?*
2. *What is the best age to begin keyboarding?*
3. *Is it still important that students learn keyboarding?*
4. *Is handwriting or keyboarding faster?*
5. *How important is it that the teacher be knowledgeable about typing?*

Here are the quick answers:

1. *Yes—emphatically*
2. *As soon as students use a computer*
3. *Of course!*
4. *That depends...*
5. *Extremely*

Don't take my word for it. Read the research.

Can K-8 Children Learn to Keyboard?

An overview of research says **yes**, elementary- and middle school-age students are cognitively, emotionally, and physically capable of learning keyboarding skills. Just as with piano and violin (and any number of sports), their fine motor skills, mental processes, and physiologic development are mature enough for the demands of typing.

> *Children often develop their own inefficient hunt-and-peck systems that take longer, waste limited computer time, and develop habits that are difficult to change.*
>
> *--Type to Learn*

Let's dig deeper.

Developmentally, some researchers maintain keyboarding is too abstract for immature brains and too demanding of undeveloped fine motor skills to learn at a young age.

Let's look at that claim. In order for keyboarding to be mastered, fingers must flow freely (Waner, Behymer, & McCrary, 1992), a concept backed by Bloom's idea of automaticity and discussed by Wronkovich (1998), who defines it as a "system of automatic habits corresponding to the system of tasks".

I agree—keyboarding requires this "system of automatic habits". Is that a reasonable expectation for K-8?

Yes and no. To ask a kindergartner (or a first/second grader) to concentrate on what each finger is doing is unreasonable and not age-appropriate. However, it is just as unreasonable to NOT expect a sixth-eighth grader to accomplish these.
The key is to introduce skills that are **age-appropriate**.

Best Age to Teach Keyboarding

Most researchers agree effective keyboarding isn't instinctual and should begin **before bad habits are created**. But when does that happen? Is elementary school too early—or too late?

Research varies on this topic. Bartholome (1996) found third grade is appropriate for touch keyboarding, but first/second graders can learn this skill with adequate instruction, a conclusion reinforced by Feutz (2001). Erthal (2002) found third graders do not possess the manual dexterity for keyboarding, and Hopkins (1998) considered fourth grade appropriate to commence formal keyboarding.

We are left with a mushy consensus among researchers of third-fifth grade as the appropriate time to begin keyboarding skills.

But fifth grade may be too late. Young children are in front of keyboards earlier than ever. In the absence of training, they will still learn, likely wrong. Therefore, logic dictates that **when students start to use computers to type, they should learn correct keyboarding practices**. With this caveat: Teach pre-keyboard skills before focusing on traditional skills.

> *...only a small proportion of classroom teachers have any formal preparation for teaching keyboarding.*
>
> *--Sormunen, 1991*

Importance of Learning Keyboarding

Many studies document the value of children learning proper typing technique (McKay, 1998; Owston, 1997; Bartholome, 1996; Bieman, 1996; Hoot, 1986). Rogers (2003) lists the following eight benefits:

1. *Improvement in language arts—reading, spelling, and writing*
2. *Improvement in efficiency using computers, thereby maximizing classroom time*
3. *Improvement in attitude—less frustration in looking for keys rather that entering information*
4. *Improvement in proper keyboarding techniques and use of the computer, thereby eliminating the formation of bad keyboarding habits for later word processing and computer applications*
5. *Improvement in motivating students toward doing schoolwork*
6. *Improvement in creative thought*
7. *Improvement in integrating keyboarding with all subject areas*
8. *Improvement in preparing students for a technological society*

Is Handwriting or Keyboarding Faster?

Students take on this question as part of the 3rd, 4th, 5th and Middle School keyboard curriculum. Several ideas:

- By considering this question in 3rd grade and examining results yearly thereafter, students realize that when they practice keyboarding, they type faster, eventually exceeding the speed they can handwrite. For those following this curriculum, it will happen in fourth-fifth grade.
- When following a course of keyboard study, student typing speed increases faster than handwriting speed. In fact, handwriting speed maxes out long before keyboarding speed does. Wikipedia claims

the average human handwrites 31 wpm on memorized text. Students in a graduated keyboarding course exceed that speed between fifth and sixth grade.

As part of the 3rd, 4th, 5th, and Middle School keyboard curriculum, students use the Scientific Method to rigorously test this question. During the research stage, students consider:

- past class results
- past personal results
- available research

When students search for background on this question, they'll find research like this:

Handwriting vs. Keyboarding—a Students' Perspective
https://askatechteacher.com/handwriting-vs-keyboarding-from-a-students-perspective/

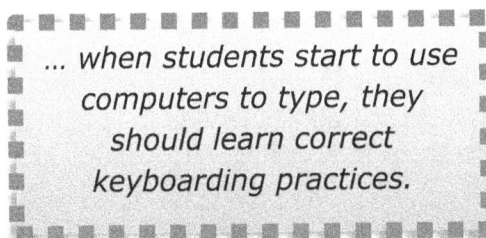

> *... when students start to use computers to type, they should learn correct keyboarding practices.*

The results of one teacher's experiment with her classes—through the students' eyes

Read these and more, but the most relevant will be the student's own experiment. Don't be surprised if that varies considerably from internet sources.

Results of this experiment are heavily dependent upon your unique student group. For example, my class results vary significantly from what I read online.

As football fans say when discussing the odds for-against their favorite team, *That's why they play the game.*

Importance of Teacher Knowledge

Sormunen's 1991 study found that classroom instructors were teaching keyboarding, but only 12% had any formal preparation in how to do that.

Condon's study (1989) found educational administrators felt elementary teachers should be provided with sufficient training to teach keyboarding. McLean (1994) suggested that instruction can be supplied by teachers who have taken a keyboarding methods course, or a business education teacher who has had elementary learning methods, or a combination of both.

Consensus of most studies indicates that a "knowledgeable" teacher is critical to help students develop appropriate techniques, as well as provide motivation and reinforcement (Nieman, 1996; Erthal, 1998).

Body/Hand Position

Seat
Chair faces keyboard, one hand's-width from the table, with keyboard one inch off edge of table.

Head and eyes
Place monitor so eyes look straight ahead with neck straight, not bent too far forward or back.

Body and Hands
Sit straight with elbows tucked against sides. Keep body natural, easy and relaxed with feet on the floor slightly apart. Keep fingers curved over keys, resting on home row.

Figure 9--Keyboarding position

Figure 10--Keyboarding posture

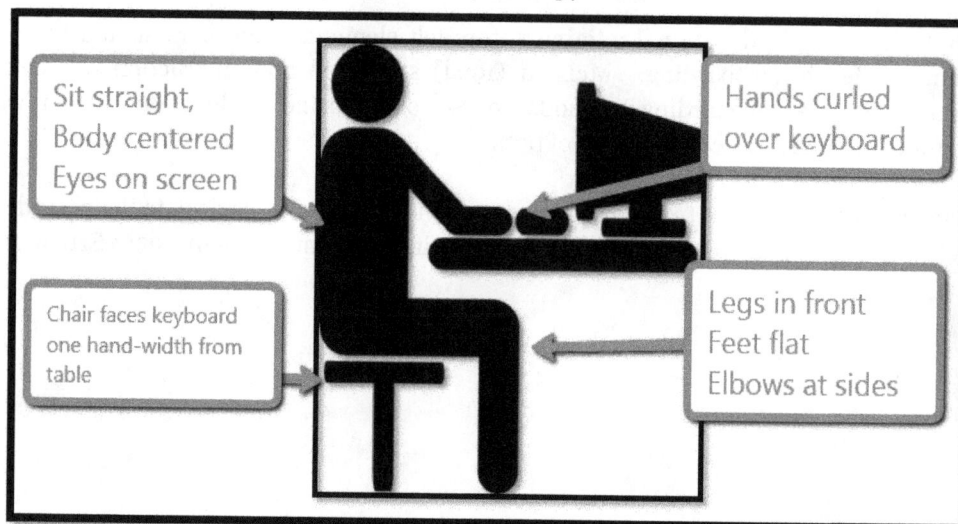

- *Elbows close to sides*
- *Fingers slightly curved over home row, pointers anchored to f and j*
- *Use finger closest to the key*
- *Move fingers, not hands; play keyboard like a piano (or violin, or guitar, or recorder). You'd never use pointer for all keys*
- *Keep hands on their own side of the keyboard, thumb on space bar*

Figure 11a-11d--Keyboarding hand positions

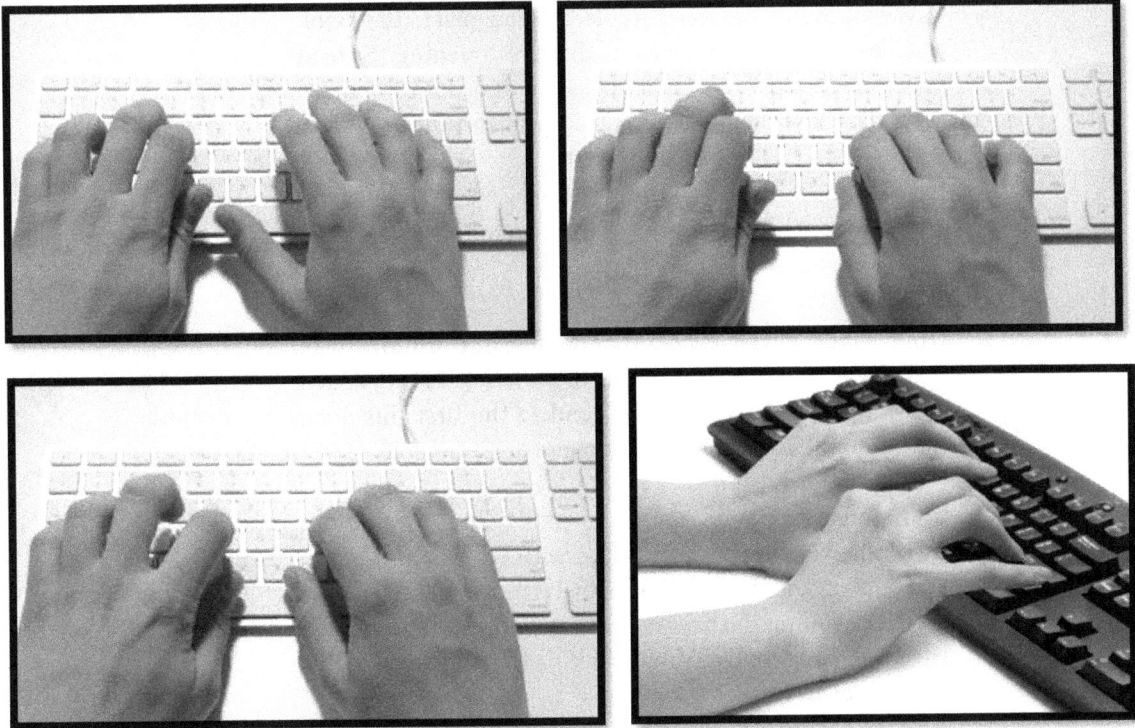

Mouse hold

Figure 12a and 12b--Mouse hand position

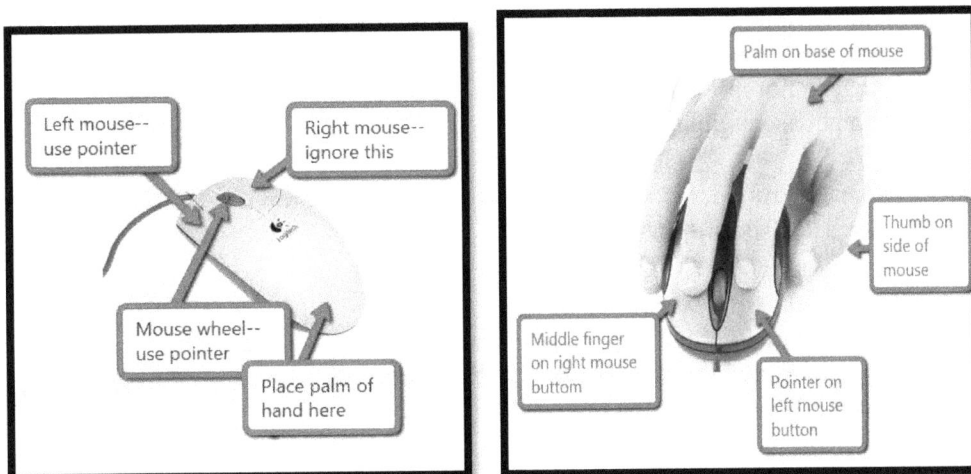

Finger Exercises

Teach finger exercises to remind students they have eight fingers and a thumb (don't use left thumb). These make keyboarding fun. Several times a month, do finger exercises to encourage use of all fingers:

Warm up Fingers

- Lay your hand flat on a table (in the inset, the book doubles as the table) with all fingers touching. Spread your fingers apart as far as possible and hold for three seconds. Close fingers together. Repeat 10 times.

- Next, lift each finger and move it around, then lower it. One at a time until you've exercised each.

Stretch Fingers

- Hold hands facing each other. Touch the thumb from your right hand to the thumb of your left hand. Touch the first finger on your right hand to the first finger on the left hand. Repeat until all fingers are touching.

- With fingers pressed together, pull palms away from each other creating a cup shape with fingers and palm. Starting at the finger tips, slowly move palms closer together, rolling the pressure down the fingers until all four fingers are pressed together. Hold for 10 seconds. Move back to the starting position and repeat 10 times.

Aerobics for Fingers

- Hold hand in the air with fingers spread apart so it looks like a "high-five." Move just the thumb to the palm and press. Bring the thumb back out to the starting position and move the first finger to the palm and press. Move the first finger back to the starting position and repeat slowly with the remaining fingers. Fingers not pressing into the palm should be held as straight as possible.

- After one round, try again a little faster. Repeat 10 times, increasing speed with each round.

Weight Training for Fingers
- Grab a scrap piece of paper and crumble it into a ball with one hand. Squeeze the paper ball tight and hold for 10 seconds. Repeat with the other hand.

Problem-solving and Keyboarding

Problem solving revolves around six areas:

- Common problems that stop students from effectively using the computer
- How to fix a broken keyboard
- How to fix hardware
- How to log on the computer
- What if the program disappeared
- Shortkeys that make accomplishing certain activities faster and easier

Common problems

Figure 13--Problem solving issues

TROUBLESHOOTING COMPUTER PROBLEMS

	Problem	Why	Solution
1.	Deleted a file	*Deleted by accident*	Open Recycle Bin—right-click--restore
2.	Can't exit a program	*Can't find X or Quit*	Alt+F4
3.	Can't find a program	*Shortcut moved*	Type 'Word' (or program name) into Search bar
4.	Keyboard doesn't work	*Unplugged, lost file*	Plug cord into back; reboot
5.	Mouse doesn't work	*Unplugged, lost file*	Plug cord into back, reboot
6.	Start button is gone	*Task bar gone*	Push Windows button
7.	No sound	*Mute on*	Unmute
		Volume down	turn volume up
		Unplugged headphones	plug headphones in
		Lost file	Reboot
8.	Can't find a file	*Saved wrong, moved*	Start button—Search
9.	Menu command grayed out	*You're in another command*	Push escape 3 times
10.	What's today's date?	*You forgot!*	Hover over the clock
11.	Taskbar gone	*Student interference*	Push Windows button
			Drag border up to expose
12.	Taskbar was moved	*Student interference*	Drag it to the bottom of screen
13.	Desktop icons messed up	*Student interference*	Right click on screen—arrange icons
			Too small? Highlight and Ctrl+ to enlarge
14.	Computer frozen	*Mouse frozen*	Reboot
15.	Program frozen	*Dialog box open*	Clear the dialog box
		Not selected on taskbar	Click program on taskbar
16.	I erased my document/text	*Ooops*	Ctrl+Z
17.	Screen says "Ctrl-Alt-Del"	*You rebooted*	Hold down Ctrl-Alt—push Delete
18.	Program closed down	*Ooops*	Is it open on the taskbar? If so—click on it
			Reopen program—see if it saved a back-up
19.	Tool bar missing on www	*Pushing F11 key*	Push F11 key
20.	Internet window too small	*Hard to read*	Ctrl+ to enlarge; Ctrl- to delarge (or Ctrl+mouse wheel)
21.	Double click doesn't work	*Who knows?*	Push enter
22.	Shift key doesn't work	*Caps lock on*	Push caps lock to disengage
23.	I can't remember how to...	*So many skills...*	Try a right click with the mouse
24.	When I type, it types over	*I want to insert text*	Push the 'insert' key
25.	The document is 'read only'	*I didn't do anything*	Just 'save-as' under a new name and all is fixed

Students know—starting in Kindergarten--that they will be expected to solve common problems similar to this list (create your list based on your unique student population—Figure 13 is a general collection). Every year, they learn a few more from the list until they know all of them.

How do I fix a broken keyboard?

You sit down to type that long project with the imminent deadline, and nothing happens. The cursor blinks... and blinks... and blinks... but goes nowhere. What do you do?

Before you buy a new keyboard, try these:

- *Is the keyboard power light on? If it is, check your screen. Is something preventing you from typing--a dialogue box that wants an answer?*

   If the light isn't on, continue down this list
- *Check plugs. Maybe the cord that connects the keyboard to the computer is loose or fell out.*
- *Reboot. Sometimes the stuff in the computer's boot-up sequence that makes the keyboard work gets lost. Restart your computer so it can re-establish itself.*
- *Do you eat at your keyboard? Doesn't everyone? I say this next solution hesitantly: Flip the keyboard over and bang on the back. Sometimes food stuck between the keys will fall out.*

None work? Throw the darn thing out and buy a new one. They don't cost much anymore.

Hardware Problems

Figure 14--Problem-solving--hardware issues

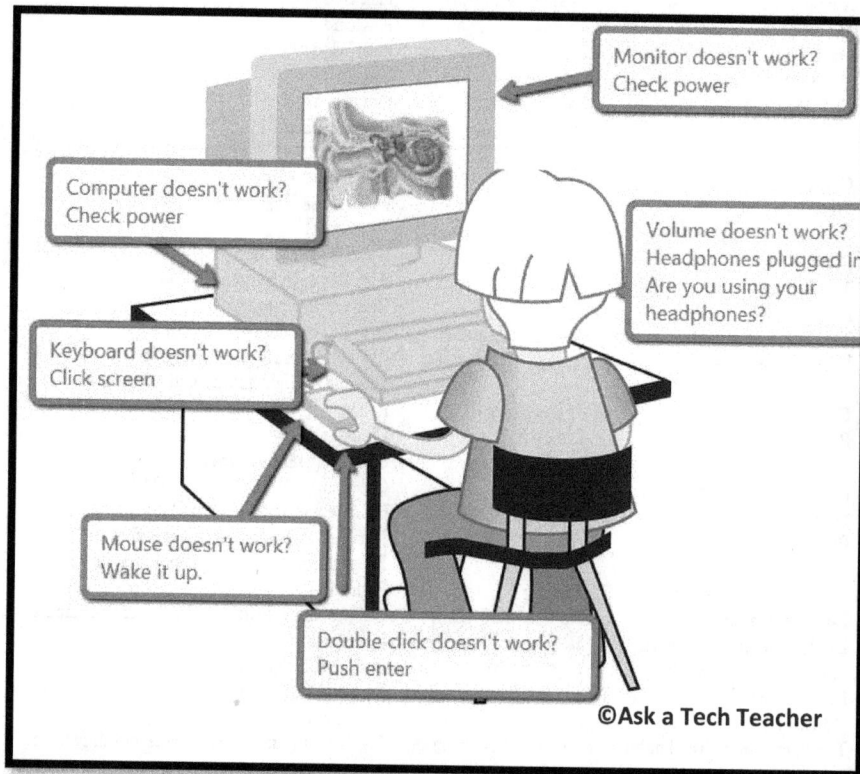

Log-in

Keyboarding starts with logging on the computer. Here's a graphic of what it takes to do this:

Figure 15--How to log in

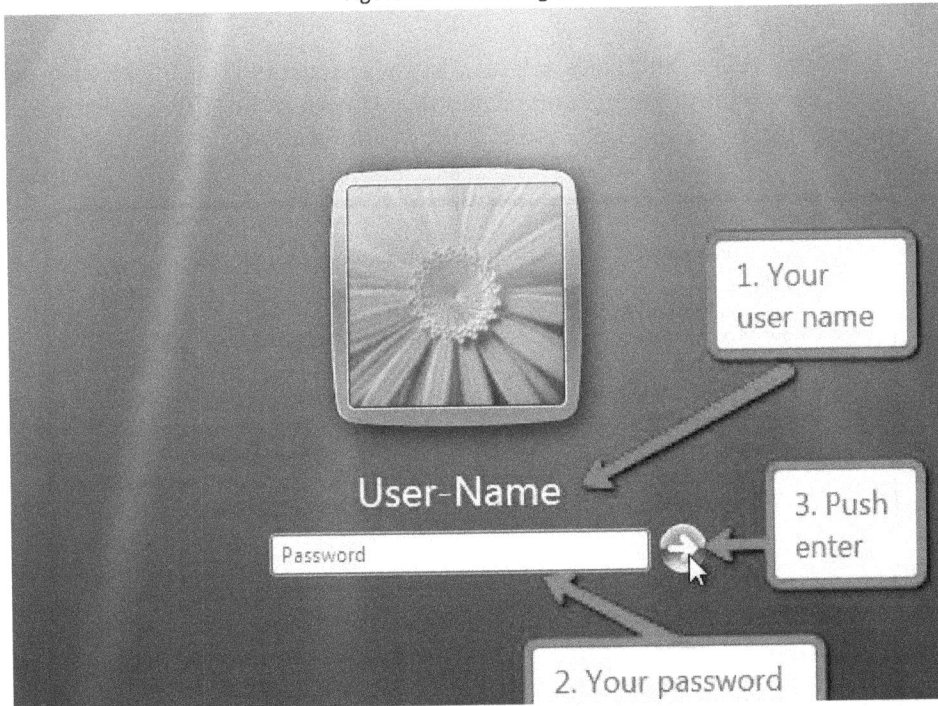

Program disappeared

If your program disappears, try two fixes before getting frustrated:

- Look around the screen—is something blocking the program access?
- Check the taskbar—is it blinking down there where it collapsed?

Figure 16--Program disappeared

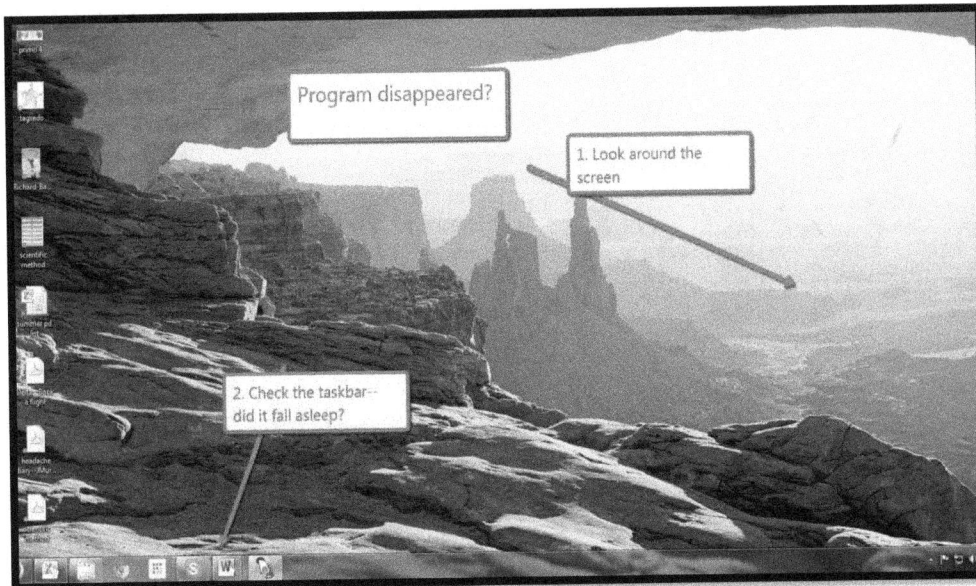

Shortkeys

As with common problems, collect shortkeys relevant to your students. You might even get them from students—quick actions they want to perform that a shortkey is perfect for. This particular list is standard shortkeys lots of students like:

Figure 17--Common shortkeys

Windows	
Maximize window	Double click title bar
Quick Exit	Alt+F4
Toggle between two windows	Alt+tab
Show start menu	WK (Windows key)
Show desktop	WK+M
Peek at your desktop	WK+spacebar
Walk through the taskbar	WK+T, WK+Tab
Open new browser tab	Click scroll on mouse
Minimize all but 1 open window	Shake win. u want (aero-shake)
Task Manager	Ctrl+Shift+Escape

General			
CTRL+C:	Copy	CTRL+L:	Left align
CTRL+X:	Cut	CTRL+R:	Right align
CTRL+V:	Paste	CTRL+B/U/I:	Bold,Unline/italic
CTRL+Z:	Undo	CTRL+or-:	Zoom in/out www
CTRL+P:	Print	CTRL+2	Double space
CTRL+K:	Add hyperlink	Shift+Alt+D/T:	Date/Time
CTRL+E:	Center align		

Website Parts

Review these website parts:

Figure 18--Website parts

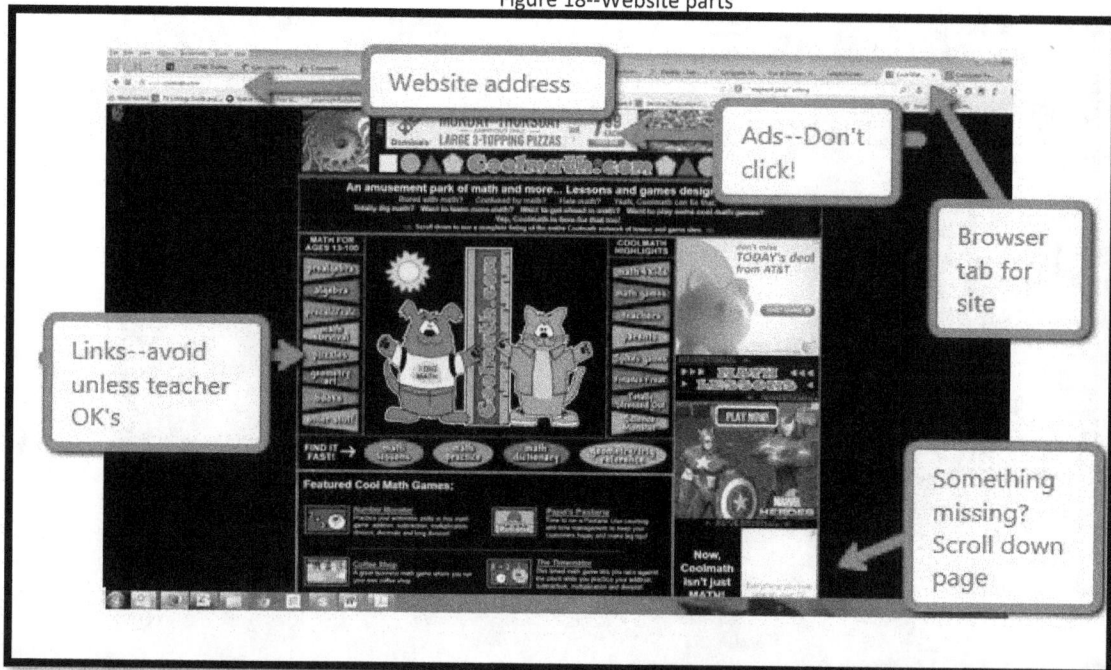

About the Publisher

Structured Learning *is the premier provider of technology resources to the education community including curricula, how-to guides, survival kits, theme-based lesson plans, Common Core materials, webinars, seminars, mentoring, coaching, posters, professional development, and one-of-a-kind online help—all to fulfill the tech demands of the 21st century classroom. Materials are classroom-tested, teacher-approved with easy-to-understand directions supported by online materials, websites, blogs, and wikis. Whether you are a new teacher wanting to do it right or a veteran educator looking for updated materials,* **Structured Learning** *and its team of technology teachers is here to assist.*

About the Authors

Ask a Tech Teacher *is a group of technology teachers who run an award-winning resource blog where they provide free materials, advice, lesson plans, pedagogic conversation, website reviews, and more to all who drop by. The free newsletters and website articles help thousands of teachers, homeschoolers, and those serious about finding the best way to maneuver the minefields of technology in education.*

Jacqui Murray *(editor and lead Ask a Tech Teacher) has been teaching K-18 technology for 20 years. She is the editor/author of over a hundred tech ed resources including a K-8 technology curriculum, K-8 keyboard curriculum, K-8 Digital Citizenship curriculum. She is an adjunct professor in tech ed, Master Teacher, webmaster for four blogs, CSTA presentation reviewer. You can find her resources at Structured Learning.*

Templates

for Blank Keyboard Quizzes (2)

Figure 19--Blank important keys template

Figure 20--Blank keyboard template

Blank Keyboard

Name: _____

©Ask a Tech Teacher

for Team Challenge

Figure 21--Team Challenge sample

ANNUAL TEAM CHALLENGE–KEYBOARD

Review

Review the following concepts. These are similar to questions that will be asked during the upcoming Team Challenge to find the summer's most tech-savvy student!

1. What's the computer log in
2. What's the computer password
3. What's your password for TTL4
4. What row do your finger start on before you even type a letter
5. What's the row above home row
6. What's the row below home row called
7. How do you find the f and j key without looking
8. Name three keys you use your pinkie to push
9. Name three keys you use your ring finger to push
10. Name three keys you use your middle finger to push
11. Name three keys you use your pointer to push
12. Name one key you use your right thumb to push
13. Which finger do you use for the backspace key
14. Which finger do you use for the shift key
15. Which finger do you use for the enter key
16. Which finger do you use for the escape key
17. What are three rules of how you sit at the keyboard
18. Do you have cat's paws or dog paws at the computer
40. What is one keyboard shortcut

19. Why (do you use cat's paws or dog paws)
20. What part of the chair do you sit on when keyboarding
21. Where are your elbows when keyboarding
22. Where does your right thumb rest when keyboarding
23. What is typing without looking at the keys called
24. Which finger pushes the a key
25. Which finger pushes the b key
26. Which finger pushes the ac key
27. Which finger pushes the d key
28. Which finger pushes the e key
29. Which finger pushes the f key
30. Which finger pushes the g key
31. Which finger pushes the h key
32. Which finger pushes the i key
33. Which finger pushes the j key
34. Which finger pushes the k key
35. What finger pushes enter
36. What's the keyboard shortcut to exit a program
37. As a general rule, which finger pushes a key
38. How do you capitalize a letter
39. As a general rule, do you fingers move or your hands in finding the keys

41. What is a desktop

Blank Hardware Quiz

Figure 22--Hardware quiz template

Your name:_____

Your teacher:_____

Name each part of the computer hardware system on the line next to it. Spelling must be correct to get credit!

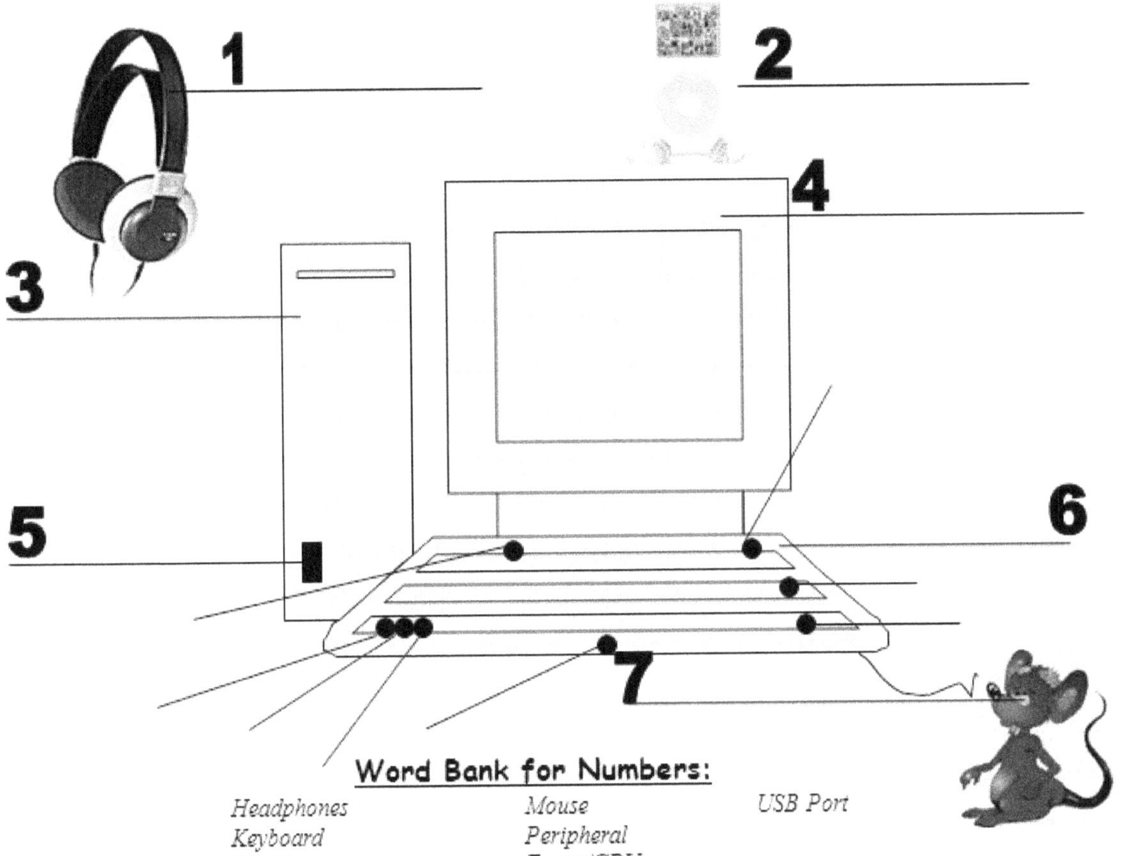

1 _____   **2** _____

4 _____

3 _____

5 _____   **6** _____

7

Word Bank for Numbers:

Headphones	Mouse	USB Port
Keyboard	Peripheral	
Monitor	Tower/CPU	

Label the keys with a circle ⬤ over them. Use this word bank:

Ctrl	Spacebar	Shift
Alt	Flying Windows	Enter
Backspace	F4	©Ask a Tech Teacher

Certificate of Achievement

THIS ACKNOWLEDGES THAT

HAS SUCCESSFULLY COMPLETED 9 MONTHS OF INTENSIVE KEYBOARDING STUDY:

- Introduction to home row
- Introduction to QWERTY row
- Introduction to lower row
- Practice with hands covered
- Digital citizenship when online

- Blank keyboard quiz (6)
- Online keyboarding
- Use of keyboarding in projects
- Introduction to word processing
- Keyboarding and online web tools

Authorized signature

Looking for Student Workbooks

Visit StructuredLearning.net

Kindergarten Check List

1st Grade Check List

2nd Grade Check List

3rd Grade Check List

4th Grade Check List

5th Grade Check List

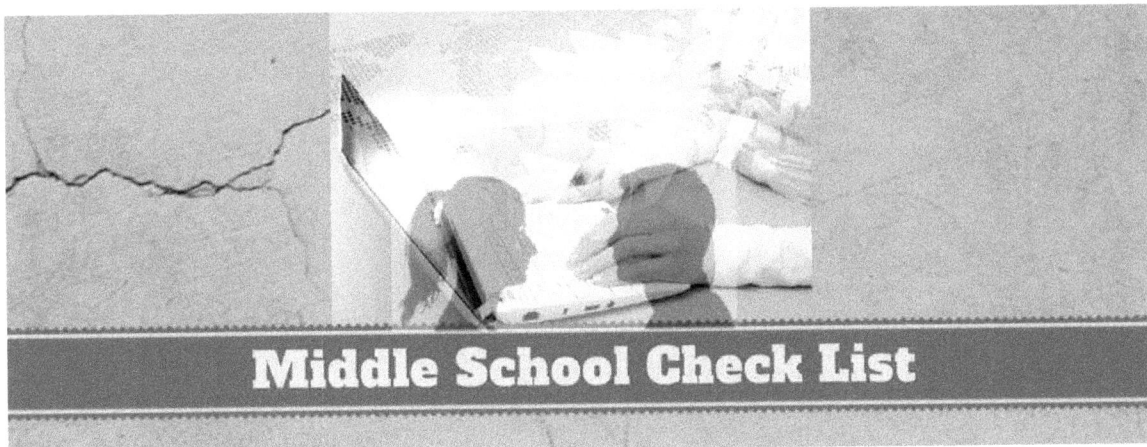

Middle School Check List

Middle School Keyboarding

Middle School GRADE

BIG IDEA

Good keyboarding skills make learning easier—projects, internet searches, online tools, web-based forms. Middle School focus: touch typing. You want to type well enough it doesn't interfere with your thoughts.

Introduction

Keyboarding is cumulative. What can be effectively learned in one grade depends heavily on earlier training. If hunt 'n peck habits become ingrained, it's difficult to keyboard effectively later.

In Middle School, students know the basics and have good habits. Their focus is touch typing--speed and accuracy. They need to think and type simultaneously. They'll practice 15-30 minutes a week at school, and 60 minutes at home (four sessions of 15 minutes each). As they complete activities, they'll check them off the month- and year-end lists.

You may want to set up a backchannel for Middle Schoolers since much keyboarding learning is done outside the classroom. Encourage them to communicate with each other about their typing lessons, share ideas, and more.

Best Practices

➢ *Students learn to type as fast as they need to*

➢ *Focus on speed and accuracy while remembering proper hand and body position*

➢ *Work on age-appropriate shortkeys*

➢ *Cover keys when practicing*

Terminology

Use keyboarding domain-specific words. Expect students to use and understand them. At the end of each month, students check the list to be sure they got them. There aren't as many as earlier years.

Posture

Students keyboard with good posture and an organized work station. When they type fast enough to keep up with their thoughts, they can change that.

Focus on Digital Citizenship

Talk about how students are responsible digital citizen every time they use the internet.

Focus on Problem Solving

Students are expected to solve common tech problems. There's a list in the introduction.

Skills learned in Middle School

- *Keyboarding*
- *Problem solving*
- *Digital citizenship*
- *Internet*

Middle School is a combination of the following keyboard activities:

- *Key memorization*
- *Covered hands during typing practice*
- *Continuous reinforcement of shortkeys*
- *Anecdotal observation by teacher of typing skills—posture, hand position, finger use, etc.*
- *Finger warm-ups*
- *Quarterly quizzes*
- *Yearly (or bi-yearly) keyboard challenge*

During each weekly lesson, do these:

- *Arrange workspace properly; follow good habits for posture and hand position*
- *Keyboard on assigned keys using preferred typing programs (software or online)*
- *Several times a month: Complete finger exercises*
- *Use keyboarding in class projects*
- *Be good digital citizens when using the internet*
- *Throughout lessons, remind students of shortkeys that accomplish oft-repeated activities*
- *Throughout lessons, remind students to attempt to solve problems before asking for help*
- *Use domain-specific terminology*
- *Keep month- and year-end skills checklist up to date*

Middle School: Month 1 week one

Vocabulary	Homework	Materials
	Type 15 minutes, four times a week, on DanceMat Typing, homerow, hands covered.	

Steps

_____In a typical keyboarding lesson:

- *Make sure workspace is arranged properly; follow good habits for posture*
- *Several times a month: use keyboarding in class projects*
- *Several times a month: complete finger exercises*
- *Every time students use the internet: discuss how to do that safely*
- *Throughout lessons, remind students to attempt to solve problems before asking for help*
- *Remind students to keep their eyes on the screen, not on hands*
- *Complete self-assessment using link provided by teacher. This may connect to Google Apps account (if students have one) or another location*

_____Set up workspace and posture.

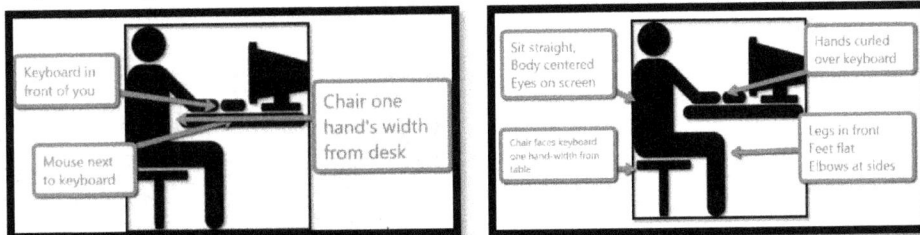

_____Review how to hold the mouse. Review parts of the computer.
_____Adapt these to school computers as well as those at home, whether it's a laptop, Chromebook, or desktop. What are the differences? Which parts can you find on an iPad?
_____Review log in.
_____Review important non-letter keys (see full-size sample under *Assessments*):

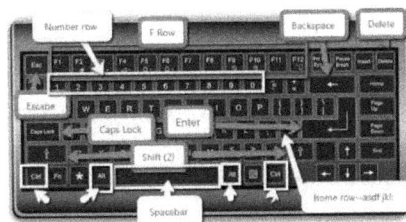

Middle School: Month 1 week two

Vocabulary	Homework	Materials
	Type 15 minutes, four times a week, on DanceMat Typing, homerow, hands covered. The goal: type without looking at hands.	*DanceMat Typing Avatar websites*

Steps

_____In a typical keyboarding lesson:

- *Make sure workspace is arranged properly; follow good habits for posture*
- *Several times a month: use keyboarding in class projects*
- *Several times a month: complete finger exercises*
- *Every time students use the internet: discuss how to do that safely*
- *Throughout lessons, remind students to attempt to solve problems before asking for help*
- *Remind students to keep their eyes on the screen, not on hands*
- *Complete self-assessment using link provided by teacher. This may connect to Google Apps account (if students have one) or another location*

_____Review website parts:

- *Website address*
- *Tabs on browser*
- *Scroll bars*
- *Ads*

_____Here's a schedule for the first three months of keyboard practice:

- *Month 1: home row*
- *Month 2: QWERTY row*
- *Month 3: lower row*

_____Use a website called DanceMat Typing (Google for address--no log-in, no fee, can be used at home and school). As students practice Home Row, hands covered, walk around and check key posture points:

- *Elbows close to sides, thumb on space bar*
- *Fingers curved, pointers anchored to f and j*

- *Fingers move, not hands*

_____Done? Create an avatar to hide student identity when you go online. Figures 23a-c are examples. Use this in class blogs (if students have one), digital portfolio, Google Apps, Instagram and other online accounts. Only the students' friends will know who it is:

- o *Voki.com*
- o *QR creator*
- o *An online (public domain) image*
- o *Another site your teacher shares*

Figure 23a-c--Avatars: Voki, image, QR code

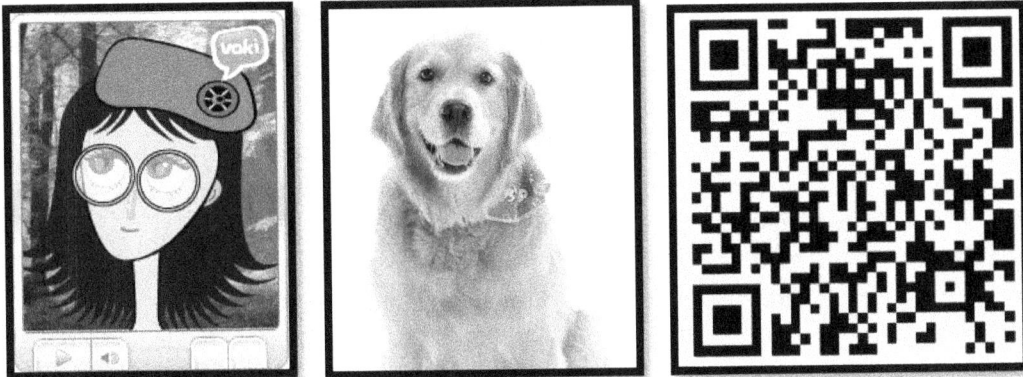

_____Before going to online sites, discuss digital rights and responsibilities:

- *digital citizenship*
- *copyrights, plagiarism*
- *fair use*
- *public domain*
- *digital footprint*
- *netiquette*
- *safe online presence*
- *safe research*

_____Remind students to use good keyboarding in projects that blend tech with learning.
_____Collaborate with grade-level teachers in using this skill authentically in their classroom.
_____Look at the Middle School Checklist and see what you can check off.

Middle School: Month 1 week three

Vocabulary	Homework	Materials
	Type 15 minutes, four times a week, on DanceMat Typing, homerow, hands covered. The goal: type without looking at hands.	*DanceMat Typing*

Steps

_____In a typical keyboarding lesson:

- *Make sure workspace is arranged properly; follow good habits for posture*
- *Several times a month: use keyboarding in class projects*
- *Several times a month: complete finger exercises*
- *Every time students use the internet: discuss how to do that safely*
- *Throughout lessons, remind students to attempt to solve problems before asking for help*
- *Remind students to keep their eyes on the screen, not on hands*
- *Complete self-assessment using link provided by teacher. This may connect to Google Apps account (if students have one) or another location*

_____Practice keyboarding for 10-15 minutes on home row, hands covered, using DanceMat Typing (Google for address).

_____Remind students to use good keyboarding in projects that blend tech with learning.

_____Collaborate with grade-level teachers in using keyboarding authentically in their classroom.

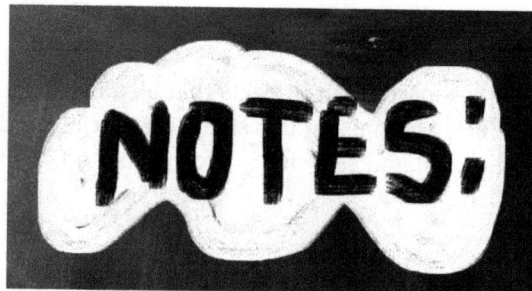

NOTES:

_____

_____

Middle School: Month 1 week four

Vocabulary	Homework	Materials
	Type 15 minutes, four times a week, on DanceMat Typing, homerow, hands covered. The goal: type without looking at hands.	*DanceMat Typing Self-assessment form*

Steps

_____In a typical keyboarding lesson:

- *Make sure workspace is arranged properly; follow good habits for posture*
- *Several times a month: use keyboarding in class projects*
- *Several times a month: complete finger exercises*
- *Every time students use the internet: discuss how to do that safely*
- *Throughout lessons, remind students to attempt to solve problems before asking for help*
- *Remind students to keep their eyes on the screen, not on hands*
- *Complete self-assessment using link provided by teacher. This may connect to Google Apps account (if students have one) or another location*

_____Practice keyboarding 10-15 minutes on home row, hands covered, on DanceMat Typing.

Ready to move on this month

If students are ready for Month 2, here's what they have accomplished:

_____*use keyboarding terms daily*
_____*sit at a computer and arrange workspace*
_____*know where important keys are on the keyboard*
_____*When student has a problem, s/he tries to solve it themselves. In fact, s/he knows the solutions to many common computer problems*
_____*know the parts of a computer and parts of a website*
_____*are a good digital citizen*
_____*practiced keyboarding on DanceMat Typing several times*
_____*submitted keyboarding homework*
_____*created an avatar and saved it, to be used on class blog, Google Apps account, or any location with personal profile*
_____*updated Middle School checklist*

Middle School: Month 2 week one

Vocabulary	Homework	Materials
	Type 15 minutes, four times a week, on DanceMat Typing, QWERTY row, hands covered. The goal: type without looking at hands.	*DanceMat Typing Speed/accuracy quiz TypingTest.com (if using this)*

Steps

_____In a typical keyboarding lesson:

- *Make sure workspace is arranged properly; follow good habits for posture*
- *Several times a month: use keyboarding in class projects*
- *Several times a month: complete finger exercises*
- *Every time students use the internet: discuss how to do that safely*
- *Throughout lessons, remind students to attempt to solve problems before asking for help*
- *Remind students to keep their eyes on the screen, not on hands*
- *Complete self-assessment using link provided by teacher. This may connect to Google Apps account (if students have one) or another location*

_____Warm up on DanceMat to prepare for today's speed and accuracy assessment.

_____This three-five minute Assessment is Part 1 of 2 (second part will be next week). Students take it every grading period. It can be completed with a word processing program like Word or Google Docs, an excerpt from a book students are reading for class, or an online site like TypingTest.com. You might switch off to adapt for different strengths among students.

_____This is a baseline to indicate the starting point; you can calculate improvement by the end of the year.

_____Do finger exercises to prepare for today's keyboarding.

_____As students type, don't stop to correct errors. After the quiz, take one minute to correct spelling errors.

_____Everyone gets 100% on this first quiz. Future grades will be based on improvement test-to-test (see intro part of book for grade scale).

20% improvement	*10/10*
10-20% improvement	*9/10*
1-10% improvement	*8/10*
No improvement	*7/10*
Slowed down	*6/10*

Grade level standards are:

3rd Grade: 15 wpm	*6th Grade: 35wpm*
4th Grade: 25 wpm	*7th Grade: 40 wpm*
5th Grade: 30 wpm	*8th Grade: 45 wpm*

_____Post a list of 'keyboard speedsters' who reached the grade level standard for speed and accuracy.

Middle School: Month 2 week two

Vocabulary	Homework	Materials
	Type 15 minutes, four times a week, on DanceMat Typing, QWERTY row, hands covered.	*DanceMat Typing Copies of quizzes*

Steps

_____In a typical keyboarding lesson:

- *Make sure workspace is arranged properly; follow good habits for posture*
- *Several times a month: use keyboarding in class projects*
- *Several times a month: complete finger exercises*
- *Every time students use the internet: discuss how to do that safely*
- *Throughout lessons, remind students to attempt to solve problems before asking for help*
- *Remind students to keep their eyes on the screen, not on hands*
- *Complete self-assessment using link provided by teacher. This may connect to Google Apps account (if students have one) or another location*

_____Keyboard 10-15 minutes, hands covered, on class keyboarding app. Stay on home and QWERTY row.
_____Students complete Part 2 of the two-step baseline assessment. Fill in blank keyboards on letter and non-letter keys (full-size sheets in *Templates*) to test knowledge of important keys
_____Students work in pairs for 10-15 minutes to complete assessment. Put both names on quizzes.
_____Cover all keyboards around the classroom.
_____Knowing key placement improves speed and accuracy.

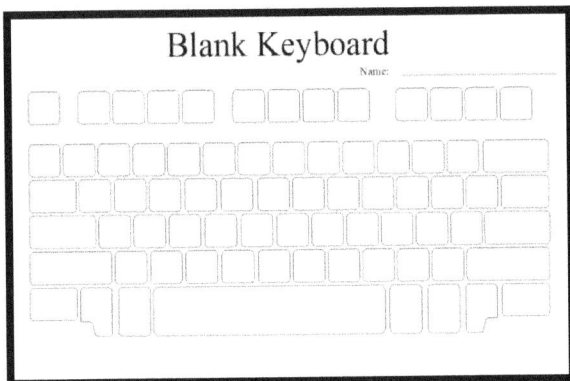

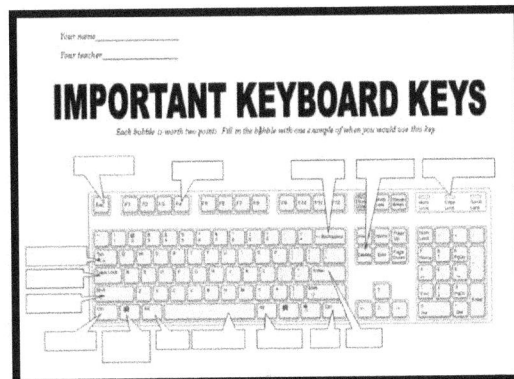

Blank Keyboard
Name:

Your name_____
Your teacher_____

IMPORTANT KEYBOARD KEYS

Each bubble is worth two points. Fill in the bubble with one example of when you would use this key

_____Remind students to use good keyboarding in projects that blend tech with learning.
_____Collaborate with grade-level teachers in using this skill authentically in their classroom.

Middle School: Month 2 week three

Vocabulary	Homework	Materials
	Type 15 minutes, four times a week, on DanceMat Typing, QWERTY row, hands covered. The goal: type without looking at hands.	*DanceMat Typing Blogs for post (if using)*

Steps

_____In a typical keyboarding lesson:

- *Make sure workspace is arranged properly; follow good habits for posture*
- *Several times a month: use keyboarding in class projects*
- *Several times a month: complete finger exercises*
- *Every time students use the internet: discuss how to do that safely*
- *Throughout lessons, remind students to attempt to solve problems before asking for help*
- *Remind students to keep their eyes on the screen, not on hands*
- *Complete self-assessment using link provided by teacher. This may connect to Google Apps account (if students have one) or another location*

_____Practice keyboarding for 10-15 minutes, hands covered, on DanceMat Typing. Stay on home and QWERTY row.

_____Students use keyboarding skills in a class project, such as to write a blog post (see Figure 24a), contribute to a Discussion Board, or tweet to class Twitter stream (see Fig. 24b):

Figure 24a and 24b—Blog post and Tweet

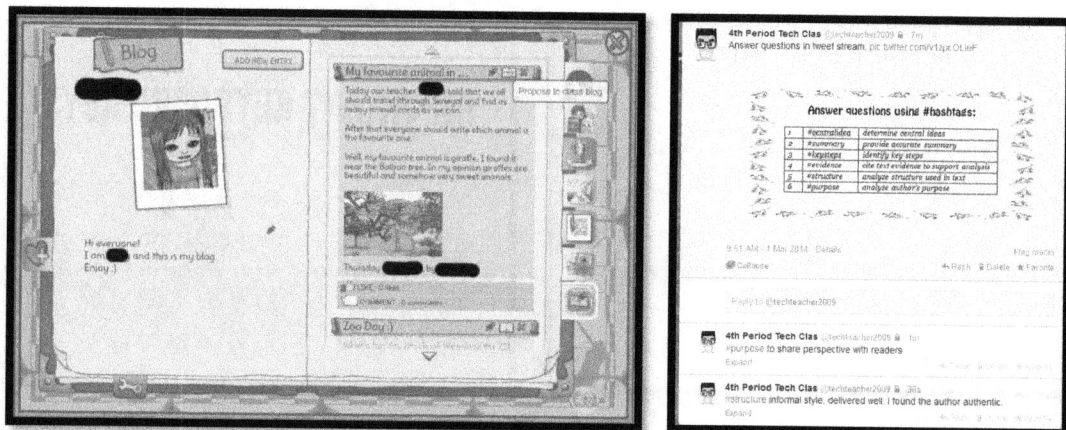

_____Share their posts or tweets and comment on those of classmates. (See Figure 25a and 25b for blog examples and 25c for Discussion Board):

Figure 25a-c—Comments to social media

_____Be sure student comments focus on the topic, use evidence to support their statements, take note of classmate's perspective (as well as others who may comment), and extend the conversation.

_____Remind students to use good keyboarding to complete project, as well as any that blend tech with learning.

_____Collaborate with grade-level teachers in using this skill authentically in their classroom.

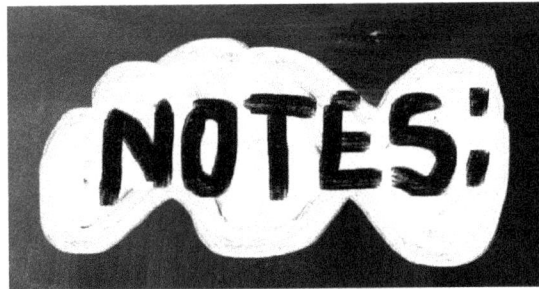

Middle School: Month 2 week four

Vocabulary	Homework	Materials
	Type 15 minutes, four times a week, on DanceMat Typing, QWERTY row, hands covered.	*DanceMat Typing*

Steps

_____In a typical keyboarding lesson:

- *Make sure workspace is arranged properly; follow good habits for posture*
- *Several times a month: use keyboarding in class projects*
- *Several times a month: complete finger exercises*
- *Every time students use the internet: discuss how to do that safely*
- *Throughout lessons, remind students to attempt to solve problems before asking for help*
- *Remind students to keep their eyes on the screen, not on hands*
- *Complete self-assessment using link provided by teacher. This may connect to Google Apps account (if students have one) or another location*

_____Practice keyboarding 10-15 minutes, hands covered, on class keyboarding app. Stay on home and QWERTY row.

Ready to move on this month

If students are ready for Month 3, here's what they have accomplished:

_____*use all terms discussed in class on a daily basis*
_____*sit at a computer and arrange workspace properly*
_____*assessed keyboarding speed, accuracy, and key placement*
_____*When student has a problem, s/he tries to solve it themselves*
_____*are a good digital citizen*
_____*practiced keyboarding on DanceMat Typing*
_____*did finger exercises*
_____*used keyboarding in a class project.*
_____*submitted keyboarding homework*
_____*updated the Middle School checklist*

Middle School: Month 3 week one

Vocabulary	Homework	Materials
	Type 15 minutes, four times a week, on DanceMat Typing, Lower row, hands covered. The goal: type without looking at hands.	*DanceMat Typing TypingTest.com Shortkeys*

Steps

_____In a typical keyboarding lesson:

- *Make sure workspace is arranged properly; follow good habits for posture*
- *Several times a month: use keyboarding in class projects*
- *Several times a month: complete finger exercises*
- *Every time students use the internet: discuss how to do that safely*
- *Throughout lessons, remind students to attempt to solve problems before asking for help*
- *Remind students to keep their eyes on the screen, not on hands*
- *Complete self-assessment using link provided by teacher. This may connect to Google Apps account (if students have one) or another location.*

popular

Shortkeys

Ctrl+F
Ctrl+S
Ctrl+P
Ctrl+Z
Ctrl+C
Ctrl+V
Ctrl+X
Ctrl+B
Ctrl+U
Ctrl+I
Ctrl+
Ctrl-

_____Practice keyboarding 10-15 minutes, hands covered, on class keyboarding app. Stay on Lower row. This is our last row-specific month. Next month, students use all keys.

_____After students practice, go to TypingTest.com or a similar online test, and assess their speed and accuracy. Students take a three-minute test and repeat once or twice. Notice how the program deducts for spelling errors and recalculates wpm.

_____Review tech problems students can solve as a group. You can do this as a contest—who knows the solution the fastest. This is similar to the year-end Teach Challenge (see *Assessment* at beginning of ebook).

_____Review shortkeys that increase typing speed (see inset). Ask students to share what other shortkeys they use. What about Ctrl+Alt+Del? What about Alt+F4? Any others they use on websites and games played at home?

Middle School: Month 3 week two

Vocabulary	Homework	Materials
	Type 15 minutes, four times a week, on DanceMat Typing, Lower row, hands covered. The goal: type without looking at hands.	*DanceMat Typing Instructions for How to Write an Ebook*

Steps

_____In a typical keyboarding lesson:

- *Make sure workspace is arranged properly; follow good habits for posture*
- *Several times a month: use keyboarding in class projects*
- *Several times a month: complete finger exercises*
- *Every time students use the internet: discuss how to do that safely*
- *Throughout lessons, remind students to attempt to solve problems before asking for help*
- *Remind students to keep their eyes on the screen, not on hands*
- *Complete self-assessment using link provided by teacher. This may connect to Google Apps account (if students have one) or another location.*

_____Practice keyboarding, hands covered, 10-15 minutes on class keyboarding app. Stay on Lower row.

_____Use keyboarding skills for a class project. For an example: Write an ebook in collaboration with LA, history, or another subject.

_____Unfortunately, it is outside the scope of this curriculum to teach word processing skills and a long-term project like writing a novel. You can find that lesson plan in the *How to Write an Ebook* (http://www.structuredlearning.net/book/write-ebook-lesson-plan/).

_____Write 1000 words at a sitting—that's about three pages (see Fig. 26):

Figure 26—1000 words

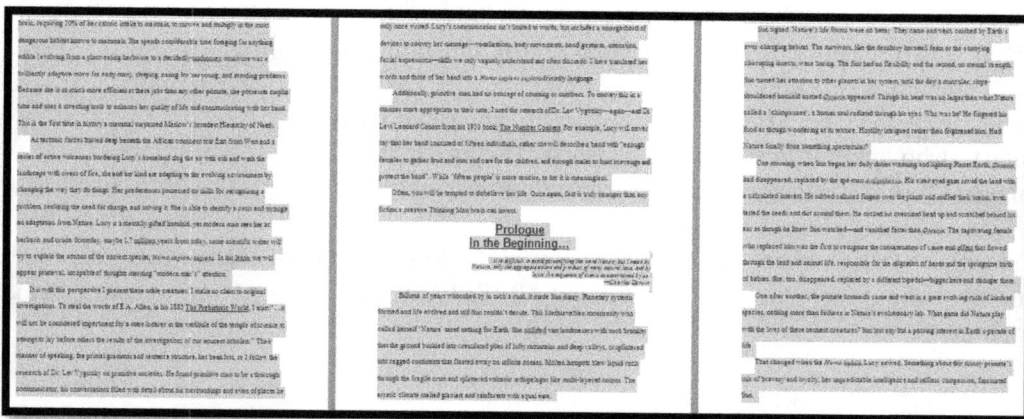

_____Encourage students to let the words tumble out, based on their research and an outline they prepared. Don't edit until the end. This project takes a full semester (or the length of a Middle School grading period). Aim for 15,000 words (technically a novella) by the time students are finished.

_____This amount of typing is fine when they are comfortable with keyboarding, aren't looking at their fingers while typing, and aren't searching for the keys that will turn thoughts into words.

Figure 27—How to write an ebook

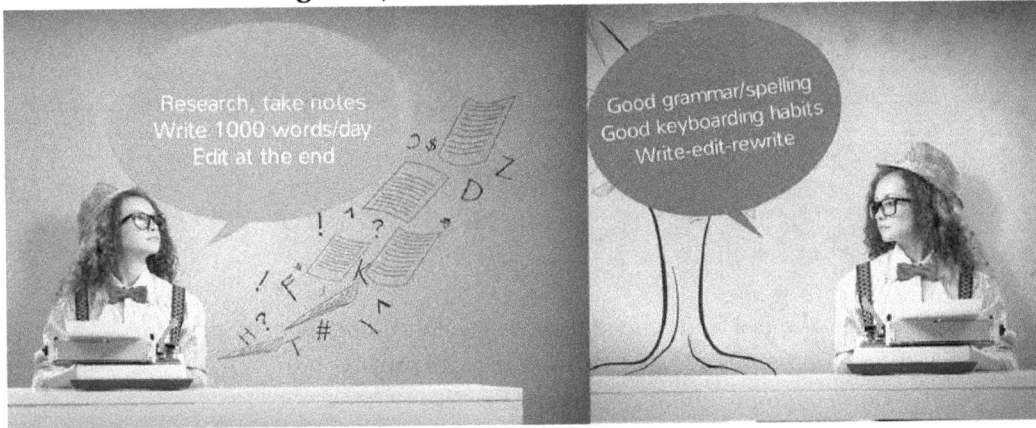

_____Use proper grammar and spelling conventions, domain-specific and academic language in story.

_____Remind students to use good keyboarding to complete this project and others that blend tech skills with learning.

_____Collaborate with grade-level teachers in using this skill authentically in their classroom.

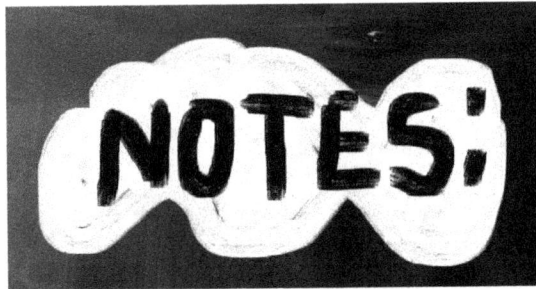

Middle School: Month 3 week three

Vocabulary	Homework	Materials
	Type 15 minutes, four times a week, on DanceMat Typing, Lower row, hands covered.	*DanceMat Typing Important keys*

Steps

_____In a typical keyboarding lesson:

- *Make sure workspace is arranged properly; follow good habits for posture*
- *Several times a month: use keyboarding in class projects*
- *Several times a month: complete finger exercises*
- *Every time students use the internet: discuss how to do that safely*
- *Throughout lessons, remind students to attempt to solve problems before asking for help*
- *Remind students to keep their eyes on the screen, not on hands*
- *Complete self-assessment using link provided by teacher. This may connect to Google Apps account (if students have one) or another location*

_____Practice keyboarding 10-15 minutes, hands covered, on class keyboarding app. Stay on Lower row.
_____Review non-letter keys. Name all twelve in eight seconds:

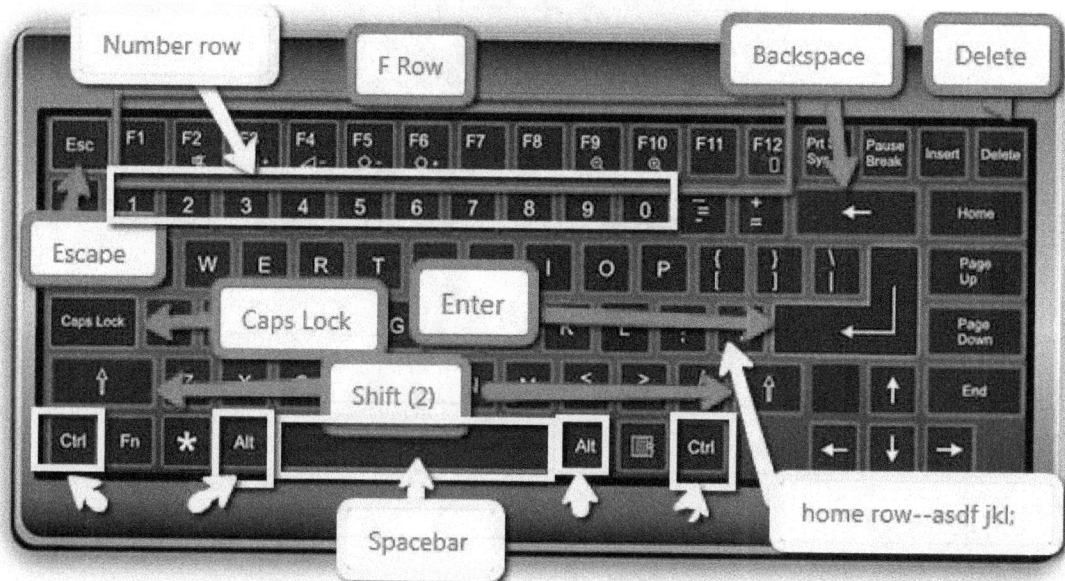

_____Remind students to use good keyboarding to complete any projects that blend tech with learning.
_____Collaborate with grade-level teachers in using this skill authentically in their classroom.

Middle School: Month 3 week four

Vocabulary	Homework	Materials
	Type 15 minutes, four times a week, on DanceMat Typing, Lower row, hands covered. The goal: type without looking at hands.	*DanceMat Typing TypingTest.com Poster webtool*

Steps

_____In a typical keyboarding lesson:

- *Make sure workspace is arranged properly; follow good habits for posture*
- *Several times a month: use keyboarding in class projects*
- *Several times a month: complete finger exercises*
- *Every time students use the internet: discuss how to do that safely*
- *Throughout lessons, remind students to attempt to solve problems before asking for help*
- *Remind students to keep their eyes on the screen, not on hands*
- *Complete self-assessment using link provided by teacher. This may connect to Google Apps account (if students have one) or another location*

_____Keyboard hands covered, 10-15 minutes on class keyboarding app. Stay on Lower row

_____Done? Check speed/accuracy on TypingTest.com.

_____Review how to use online sites safely.

_____Use an online poster creator to share a quote or information with classmates. See Figure 28a-c for examples. If you need suggestions, check the Ask a Tech Teacher resource pages.

_____Keep it simple: text overlaid on a nice image. Use good keyboarding habits, and check grammar and spelling before sharing.

Figure 28a-c--Posters in Canva

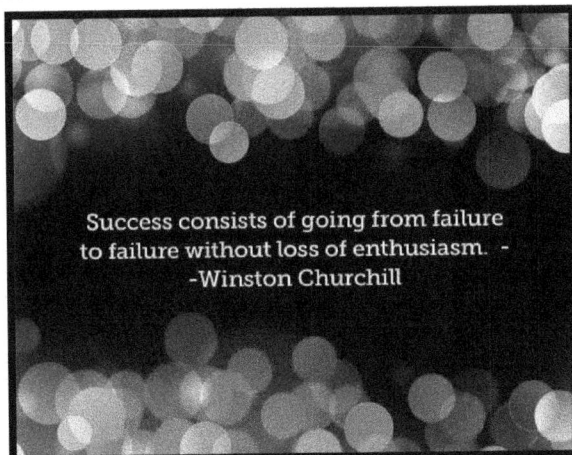

stay in the digital neighborhood
Respect copyrights
Avoid ads

On the internet, do not give out your name or personal information

Success consists of going from failure to failure without loss of enthusiasm. -
-Winston Churchill

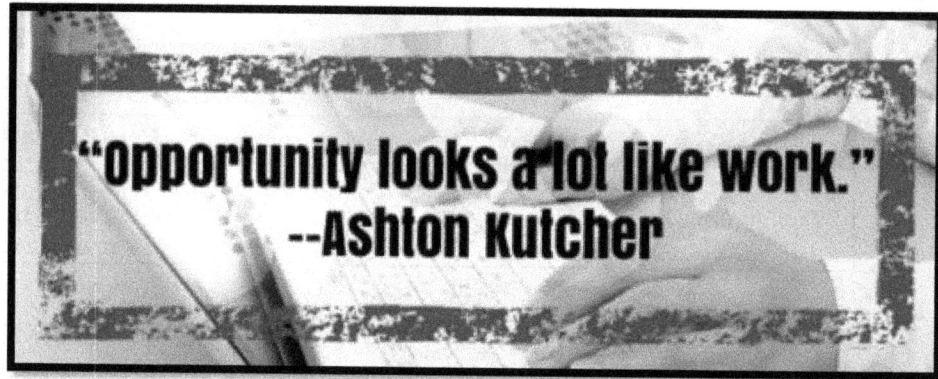

_____Next: Use an online 'fake' site to generate text chat (Figure 29a using iFakeText.com) or a newspaper clipping (Figure 29b using Fodey.com) that supports a topic in one of students' classes. Treat this as an assessment of knowledge on that issue—don't research, just type from memory:

Figure 29a—Fake chat; Figure 29b—Fake newspaper

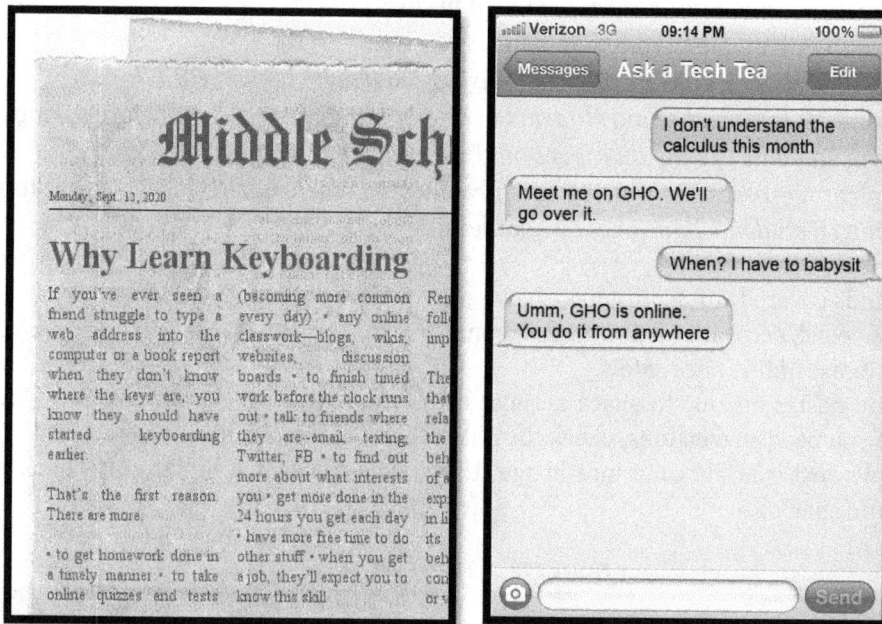

_____Done? Share a screen shot to student blog, class wiki, or another location accessible to classmates.
_____Remind students to use good keyboarding to complete all projects that blend tech with learning.
_____Collaborate with grade-level teachers in using this skill authentically in their classroom.

Ready to move on this month

If students are ready for Month 4, here's what they have accomplished:

_____*use keyboarding terms daily*
_____*sit at a computer and arrange workspace correctly*

_____know where important keys are on the keyboard
_____When students have a problem, they try to solve it before asking for help
_____are a good digital citizen
_____practiced keyboarding on DanceMat Typing several times
_____used keyboarding in several class projects
_____submitted your keyboarding homework
_____updated Middle School checklist

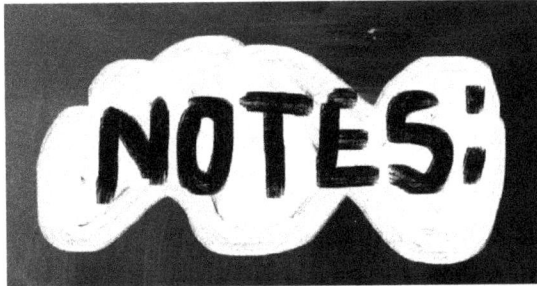

NOTES:

_____

_____

_____

_____

_____

_____

_____

_____

_____

Middle School: Month 4 week One-four

Vocabulary	Homework	Materials
	Type 15 minutes, four times a week, hands covered, on a progressive keyboard program. The goal: type without looking at hands.	*Progressive keyboarding program* *Comic creator*

Steps

_____In a typical keyboarding lesson:

- *Make sure workspace is arranged properly; follow good habits for posture*
- *Several times a month: use keyboarding in class projects*
- *Several times a month: complete finger exercises*
- *Every time students use the internet: discuss how to do that safely*
- *Complete self-assessment using link provided by teacher. This may connect to Google Apps account (if students have one) or another location*

_____Switch to a progressive keyboarding program that will track student progress. If you don't have a class favorite, check the Ask a Tech Teacher resource pages. Continue with this program the rest of the year. Students cover hands while practicing. I provide cloths they use at school and take home if they'd like. It feels hard at first and quickly becomes easier. Focus is speed and accuracy.

_____As students type, observe posture, hand position, eye placement. Make suggestions to the class when you see an endemic problem.

_____Practice keyboarding with class projects like a story, an essay, a biography, a topical magazine. For example: Create a comic using an online tool—you can find suggestions on Ask a Tech Teacher resource pages.

Figure 30a and 30b—Comic creators—two samples

_____Make it appropriate to task and audience; include images, text, design elements.

Figure 31—Comic creator II

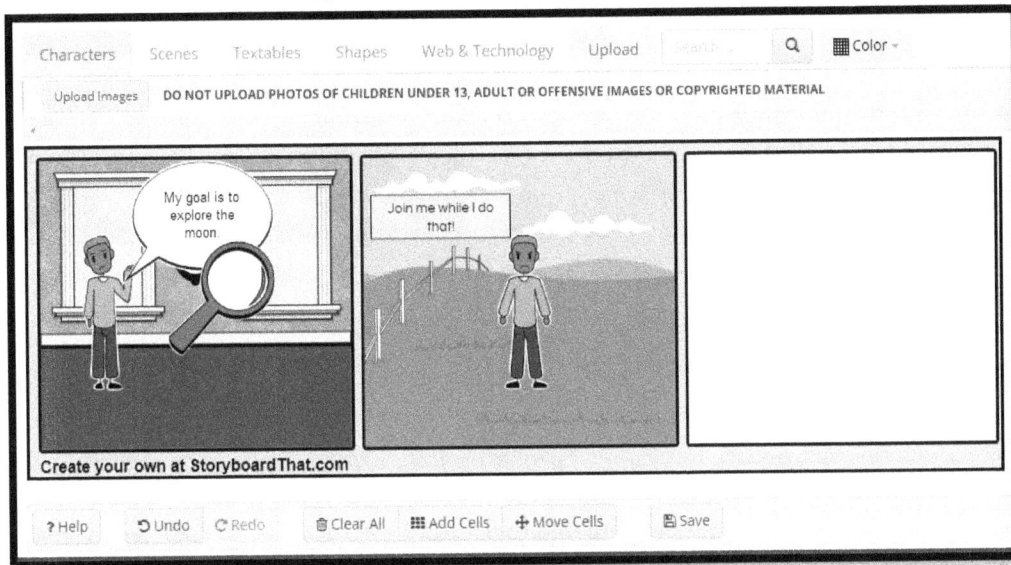

_____Remind students to use good keyboarding in any projects that blend tech with learning.
_____Collaborate with grade-level teachers in using this skill authentically in their classroom.
_____Notice how much easier it is to type when you know where keys are.
_____Save project to your digital portfolio.

Ready to move on this month

If students are ready for Month 5, here's what they have accomplished:

_____*use keyboarding terms daily*
_____*sit at a computer correctly*
_____*know where important keys are*
_____*try to solve problems themselves before requesting help*
_____*are a good digital citizen*
_____*practiced keyboarding several times*
_____*used keyboarding in several class projects*
_____*submitted keyboarding homework*
_____*updated Middle School checklist*

Middle School: Month 5 week One-four

Vocabulary	Homework	Materials
	Type 15 minutes, four times a week, hands covered, on a progressive keyboard program	*Keyboarding program* *Blank keyboard quizzes*

Steps

_____In a typical keyboarding lesson:

- *Make sure workspace is arranged properly; follow good habits for posture*
- *Several times a month: use keyboarding in class projects*
- *Several times a month: complete finger exercises*
- *Every time students use the internet: discuss how to do that safely*
- *Throughout lessons, remind students to attempt to solve problems before asking for help*
- *Remind students to self-assess using the spreadsheet you provided*
- *Remind students to keep their eyes on the screen, not on hands*
- *Complete self-assessment using link provided by teacher. This may connect to Google Apps account (if students have one) or another location*

_____Continue keyboard practice on a progressive typing program. Students cover hands while practicing. It feels hard at first and quickly becomes easier. The focus is on speed and accuracy.

_____Review key placement. Find twelve keys in eight seconds:

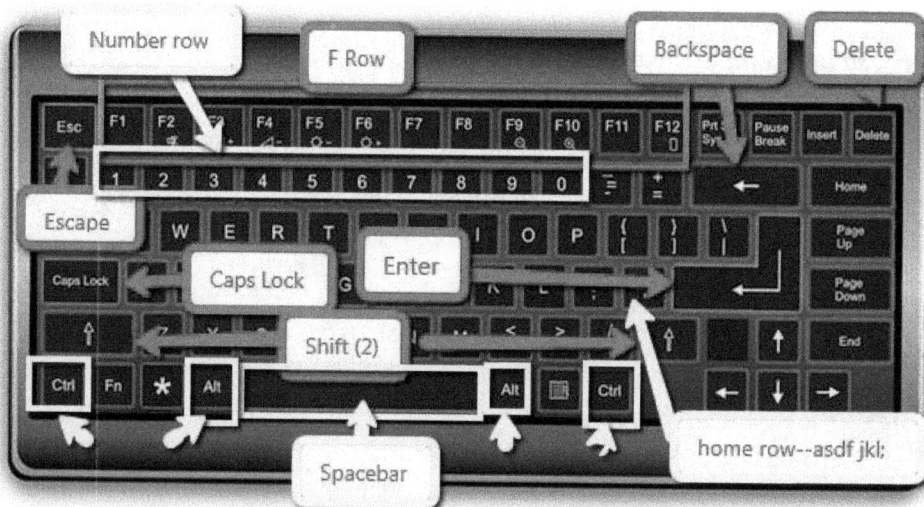

_____Review computer problem-solving (Figure 32):

Figure 32--Trouble-shooting Computer Problems

TROUBLESHOOTING COMPUTER PROBLEMS

	Problem	Why	Solution
1	Deleted a file	Deleted by accident	Open Recycle Bin—right-click--restore
2.	Can't exit a program	Can't find X or Quit	Alt+F4
3.	Can't find a program	Shortcut moved	Type 'Word' (or program name) into Search bar
4.	Keyboard doesn't work	Unplugged, lost file	Plug cord into back; reboot
5.	Mouse doesn't work	Unplugged, lost file	Plug cord into back, reboot
6.	Start button is gone	Task bar gone	Push Windows button
7.	No sound	Mute on	Unmute
		Volume down	turn volume up
		Unplugged headphones	plug headphones in
		Lost file	Reboot
8.	Can't find a file	Saved wrong, moved	Start button—Search
9.	Menu command grayed out	You're in another command	Push escape 3 times
10.	What's today's date?	You forgot!	Hover over the clock
11.	Taskbar gone	Student interference	Push Windows button
			Drag border up to expose
12.	Taskbar was moved	Student interference	Drag it to the bottom of screen
13.	Desktop icons messed up	Student interference	Right click on screen—arrange icons
			Too small? Highlight and Ctrl+ to enlarge
14.	Computer frozen	Mouse frozen	Reboot
15.	Program frozen	Dialog box open	Clear the dialog box
		Not selected on taskbar	Click program on taskbar
16.	I erased my document/text	Ooops	Ctrl+Z
17.	Screen says "Ctrl-Alt-Del"	You rebooted	Hold down Ctrl-Alt—push Delete
18.	Program closed down	Ooops	Is it open on the taskbar? If so—click on it
			Reopen program—see if it saved a back-up
19.	Tool bar missing on www	Pushing F11 key	Push F11 key
20.	Internet window too small	Hard to read	Ctrl+ to enlarge; Ctrl- to delarge (or Ctrl+mouse wheel)
21.	Double click doesn't work	Who knows?	Push enter
22.	Shift key doesn't work	Caps lock on	Push caps lock to disengage
23.	I can't remember how to...	So many skills...	Try a right click with the mouse
24.	When I type, it types over	I want to insert text	Push the 'insert' key
25.	The document is 'read only'	I didn't do anything	Just 'save-as' under a new name and all is fixed

_____Take Part 1 of 2 of the second Keyboarding Assessment of school year: It is a three-five minute speed and accuracy Assessment (like last time).

_____Loosen up with finger exercises.

_____Open a word processing program like Word or Google Docs to type a sample from a book being read in class. Optionally, use a website like TypingTest.com.

_____As students take the timed test, observe them to offer a formative assessment of their skills.

_____After the quiz, students correct spelling.

_____Unfortunately, it is outside the scope of this curriculum to teach word processing skills. You can find a full Middle School tech curriculum here: http://www.structuredlearning.net/book/k-8-tech-curriculum-set/.

_____Students grades are based on improvement test-to-test:

- 20% improvement   10/10
- 10-20% improvement   9/10
- 1-10% improvement   8/10
- No improvement   7/10
- Slowed down   6/10

_____Grade level standards are:

6th Grade:	35wpm
7th Grade:	40 wpm
8th Grade:	45 wpm

_____Post a list of students who reached the speed and accuracy grade level standard.

_____Another week this month: Students work in pairs for 10-15 minutes to complete Part 2 of the keyboarding assessment—fill in two blank keyboards of important keys:

_____Cover visible keyboards before beginning.

_____Grading will be based on the same criteria used for the speed/accuracy quiz—it will depend upon improvement from earlier quizzes.

_____Remind students to use good keyboarding to complete projects that blend tech with learning.

_____Collaborate with grade-level teachers in using this skill authentically in their classroom.

_____Key placement becomes speed and accuracy.

Ready to move on this month

If students are ready for Month 6, here's what they have accomplished:

_____*use keyboarding terms daily*

_____*sit at a computer and arrange your workspace correctly*

_____*You know where important keys are on the keyboard*

_____*When students have a problem, they try to solve it themselves before requesting help*

_____*are a good digital citizen*

_____*practiced keyboarding several times*

_____*did finger exercises several times*

_____*submitted homework as suggested by your teacher*

_____*completed the two-step keyboarding assessment*

_____*updated Middle School checklist*

Middle School: Month 6 week One-four

Vocabulary	Homework	Materials
	Type 15 minutes, four times a week, hands covered, on a progressive keyboard program. The goal: type without looking at hands.	*Progressive typing program* *Writing prompt* *School's Scientific Method*

Steps

_____In a typical keyboarding lesson:

- *Make sure workspace is arranged properly; follow good habits for posture*
- *Several times a month: use keyboarding in class projects*
- *Several times a month: complete finger exercises*
- *Every time students use the internet: discuss how to do that safely*
- *Throughout lessons, remind students to attempt to solve problems before asking for help*
- *Remind students to keep their eyes on the screen, not on hands*
- *Complete self-assessment using link provided by teacher. This may connect to Google Apps account (if students have one) or another location*

_____Practice keyboarding, hands covered, on a progressive typing program. Focus on speed and accuracy.
_____This is the hand look you strive for:

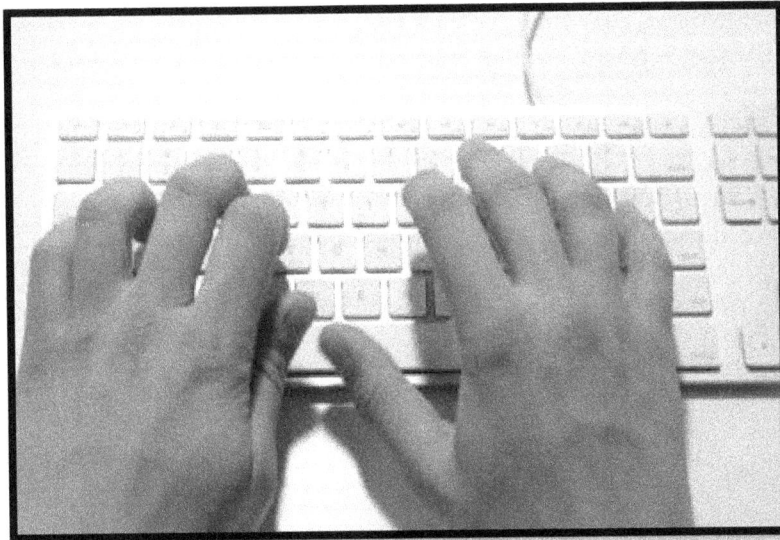

_____This month: Assess typing vs. handwriting speed by circling back on the scientific method (Figure 33):

Figure 33—Scientific method

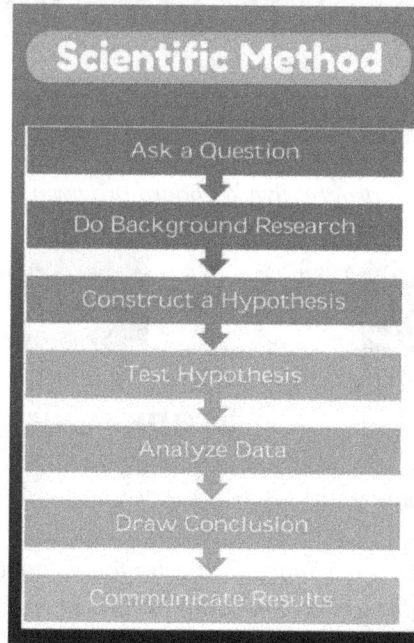

Note: There are varying examples of the scientific method in Middle School. Talk to the science teacher and adapt this experiment to the one s/he uses.

_____What were the results last year? Do students remember that most typed faster than they handwrote? Do they think this has changed?

_____Discuss the Scientific Method, its steps, applicability to general problem solving (such as this issue).

_____Now follow these steps (see *Research* for more detail):

- **Ask a question**: Is handwriting or keyboarding faster?
- **Do background research:** Discuss whether handwriting is faster/slower than typing.
- **Construct a hypothesis:** Something like: *Students in Mr. X's class type faster than they handwrite.*
- **Test hypothesis**: Do an experiment to see which is faster—handwriting or typing. Students handwrite their typed speed quiz for the same length of time they typed (three-five minutes).
- **Analyze data:** Each student compares his/her handwriting and typing speed. Which is faster? Compare personal findings to classmates'. Why are some students faster and others slower? What were some problems faced in handwriting for three-five minutes:

  - *Pencil lead broke*
  - *Eraser gone*
  - *Hands got tired*
  - *It got boring*

- **Draw conclusions**: What can be decided based on results?

- **Communicate results:** Share with other classes. At what grade level do students consistently type faster than they handwrite? Why?

_____For the non-written text, give students a prompt. Mentally, they build a five-paragraph essay (or one that follows your school's writing guidelines)—1) introduction, 2-4) one paragraph per point, 5) conclusion. Take a minute to think this through, and then write from memory.

_____Is that harder? Did it change the results?

_____Post a list of students who type faster than they handwrite.

Ready to move on this month

If students are ready to go to Month 7, here's what they have accomplished:

_____*use keyboarding terms daily*

_____*sit at a computer and arrange workspace correctly*

_____*know where important keys are on the keyboard*

_____*When students have a problem, s/he tries to solve it themselves before requesting help*

_____*are a good digital citizen*

_____*practiced keyboarding*

_____*did finger exercises several times this month*

_____*completed keyboarding assessment*

_____*submitted keyboarding homework*

_____*updated Middle School checklist*

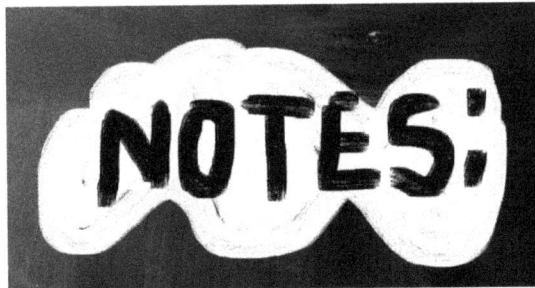

NOTES:

_____

_____

_____

_____

_____

Middle School: Month 7 week One-four

Vocabulary	Homework	Materials
	Type 15 minutes, four times a week, hands covered, on a progressive keyboard program. The goal: type without looking at hands.	*Progressive keyboarding program TypingTest.com ASCII art*

Steps

_____In a typical keyboarding lesson:

- *Make sure workspace is arranged properly; follow good habits for posture*
- *Several times a month: use keyboarding in class projects*
- *Several times a month: complete finger exercises*
- *Every time students use the internet: discuss how to do that safely*
- *Throughout lessons, remind students to attempt to solve problems before asking for help*
- *Complete self-assessment using link provided by teacher. This may connect to Google Apps account (if students have one) or another location*

_____Practice keyboarding, hands covered, on a progressive program. Addresses are provided earlier in this book—or Google. Focus is on speed and accuracy.

_____Observe students as they type and evaluate their errors. The cause of the error is often more important than the fact that the student made a mistake. Many errors are symptoms of faulty keyboarding technique, wrong finger curve, eyes not on copy, or posture:

- *Errors such as reversals, typing an "e" instead of an "r", and omission or addition of letters are often due to poor planning or thinking rather than inaccurate finger placement*
- *Other causes of errors include tension, wandering attention, faulty reading, wrong mind set*
- *Watch students for signs of fatigue, moving heads, massaging, or tight facial expressions*

_____Done? Have students check speed and accuracy on TypingTest.com.

_____Introduce **ASCII Art**—amazing computer drawings where letters become pictures. Done well, ASCII Art never fails to impress viewers with the student's consummate keyboarding skills.

_____Here's a simple way to do this:

- *Add a watermark of a picture to MS Word or another word processing program. A single image works best. See Figure 37b and 38a for examples.*
- *Type over it with appropriate letters, numbers and symbols to provide depth.*
- *Change color of specific letters/symbols to add depth (see Figure 38a—pumpkin).*
- *Delete the watermark so all that's left is typed letters/numbers/symbols.*

- *How long does this take? About twenty minutes.*

_____ It can be simple or sophisticated. Figure 34c—a robotics unit; Figure 35b—Civil War:

Figure 34a—ASCII Art; Figure 34b-c—ASCII Art before and after

Figure 35a and 35b—ASCII Art—Lincoln before and after

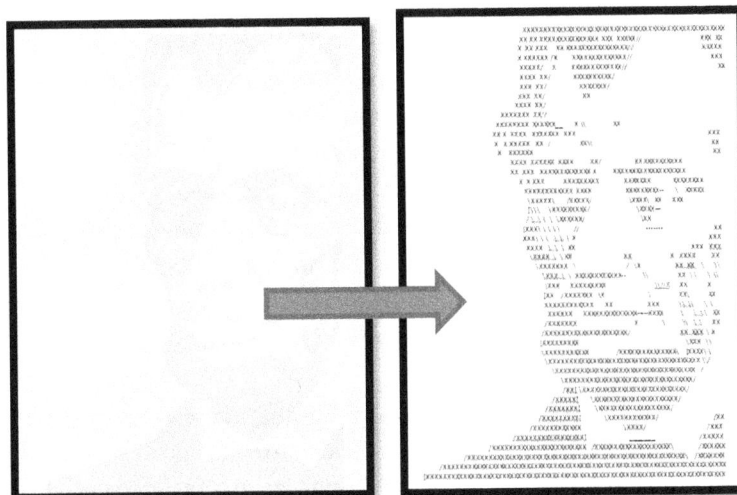

_____Remind students to use good keyboarding to complete projects that blend tech with learning.
_____Collaborate with grade-level teachers in using this skill authentically in their classroom.

Ready to move on this month

If students are ready for Month 8, here's what they have accomplished:

_____*use keyboarding terms daily*
_____*arrange workspace correctly; know where important keys are*
_____*When students have a problem, they try to solve it before requesting help*
_____*are a good digital citizen*
_____*practiced keyboarding several times*
_____*did finger exercises this month*
_____*submitted homework*
_____*used keyboarding (for example, ASCII art) in a project from another class*
_____*updated year-end grade checklist*

Middle School: Month 8 week One-four

Vocabulary	Homework	Materials
	Type 15 minutes, four times a week, hands covered, on a progressive keyboard program. The goal: type without looking at hands.	*Progressive keyboarding program* *Note-taking tool*

Steps

_____In a typical keyboarding lesson:

- *Make sure workspace is arranged properly; follow good habits for posture*
- *Several times a month: use keyboarding in class projects*
- *Several times a month: complete finger exercises*
- *Every time students use the internet: discuss how to do that safely*
- *Throughout lessons, remind students to attempt to solve problems before asking for help*
- *Remind students to keep their eyes on the screen, not on hands*
- *Complete self-assessment using link provided by teacher. This may connect to Google Apps account (if students have one) or another location*

_____Keyboard, hands covered, on a progressive program. Website addresses are found earlier in this book—or Google. Students cover hands while practicing. Focus on speed and accuracy.

_____Use keyboarding to take notes in class. If you don't have a favorite digital notetaking took, check the Ask a Tech Teacher resource pages.

_____Any note-taking option is fine—your school may have an account with one. What is important is that while students type notes, they use good keyboarding skills.

_____When done, share notes with classmates.

_____See Figure 37a for an example in Evernote, Figure 37b for an example in Notability (for iPads), and Figure 36 for Google Apps:

Figure 36—Keyboarding in note-taking II

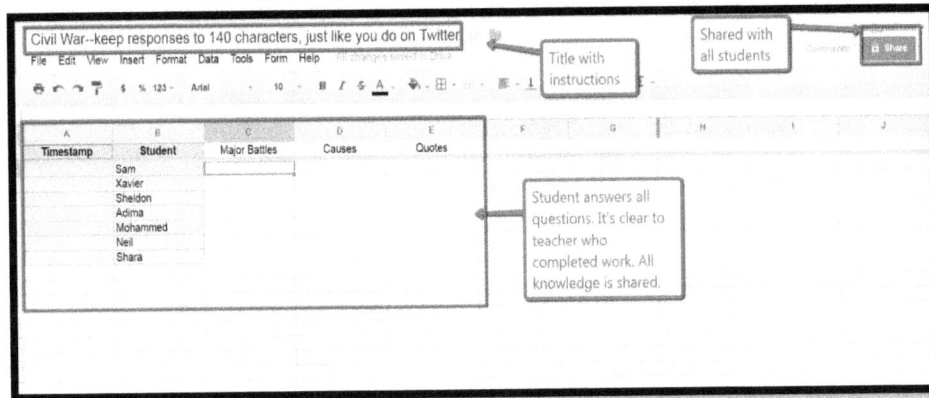

Figure 37a and 37b—Keyboarding in Evernote and Notability

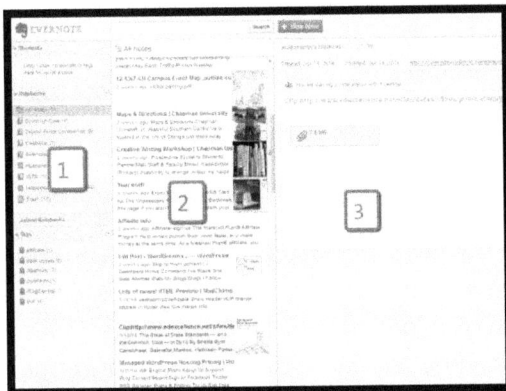

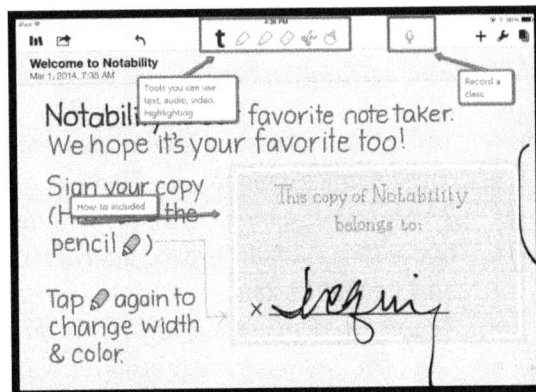

_____Remind students to use good keyboarding to complete projects that blend tech with learning.
_____Collaborate with grade-level teachers in using this skill authentically in their classroom.

Ready to move on this month

If students are ready for Month 9, here's what they have accomplished:

_____*use keyboarding terms daily as you keyboard*
_____*sit at a computer and arrange workspace correctly*
_____*When student has a problem, s/he tries to solve it themselves*
_____*know the parts of a computer and parts of a website*
_____*are a good digital citizen*
_____*practiced keyboarding several times*
_____*did finger exercises several times*
_____*submitted homework*
_____*took notes during class using good keyboarding skills*
_____*updated Middle School checklist*

Middle School: Month 9 week One-four

Vocabulary	Homework	Materials
	Type 15 minutes, four times a week, hands covered, on a progressive keyboard program. The goal: type without looking at hands.	*Progressive keyboarding program* *Keyboard assessment quizzes* *Certificates of Achievement*

Steps

_____In a typical keyboarding lesson:

- *Make sure workspace is arranged properly; follow good habits for posture*
- *Several times a month: use keyboarding in class projects*
- *Several times a month: complete finger exercises*
- *Every time students use the internet: discuss how to do that safely*
- *Throughout lessons, remind students to attempt to solve problems before asking for help*
- *Remind students to keep their eyes on the screen, not on hands*
- *Complete self-assessment using link provided by teacher. This may connect to Google Apps account (if students have one) or another location*

_____Keyboard, hands covered, on a progressive program. Links provided earlier in this book—or Google).

_____One week: Take the final Keyboard Assessment, Part 1 (second part will be next week). It can be completed in a word processing program like MS Word or Google Docs, using a sample provided by your teacher, or by going to a website like TypingTest.com.

_____As students type, observe strong and weak points to share with students.

_____After quiz, students take a minute to correct spelling.

_____Grade level standards are:

Figure 34--Poster on keyboarding'

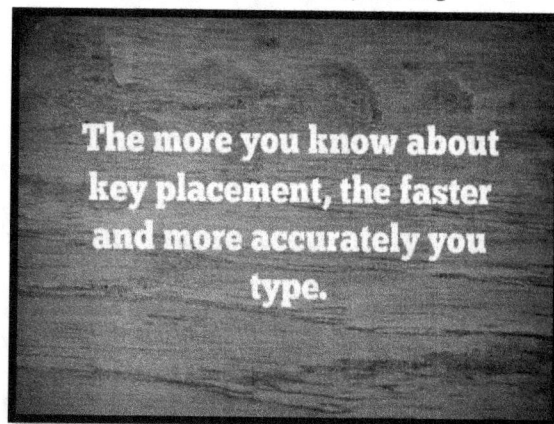

The more you know about key placement, the faster and more accurately you type.

6th Grade:	*35wpm*
7th Grade:	*40 wpm*
8th Grade:	*45 wpm*

_____Grade will depend upon improvement:

- *20% improvement*   *10/10*
- *10-20% improvement*   *9/10*

- *1-10% improvement*   *8/10*
- *No improvement*   *7/10*
- *Slowed down*   *6/10*

_____Post a list of 'keyboard speedsters' of students who reached the grade level standard for speed and accuracy.

_____Another week this month: Take Part 2 of assessment. Work in pairs for 10-15 minutes to fill in two blank keyboards. Cover visible keyboards in room.

_____Key placement knowledge translates to speed and accuracy.

Figure 39--Sample Certificate of Achievement

_____The last class of this last month, students participate in a keyboarding Team Challenge (see more details at beginning of book, under *Assessment*). Working with classmates, they develop a list of questions that address keyboarding skills

_____Keyboarding skill is knowing keys AND finding them automatically, without thinking. In this Challenge, students are expected to give answers immediately after the question is asked—no thinking!

_____Break class into teams. The moderator asks a question from the list and the team gets three seconds to answer verbally or with the correct finger. When time runs out, the team with the most points is the winner.

_____Award year-end Certificates of Achievement for students who finished all items in the grade-level checklist (see Figure 39 for sample. Full size in *Assessments*).

Ready to move on

To determine if students are ready for the next grade level, go over the checklist at end of this unit and see if everything checked off. Can students complete all skills?

Middle School Check List

To graduate to the next keyboarding level, student must have the following skills checked off:

Posture

_____*Legs in front, body in front, elbows at sides*
_____*Chair one hand-width from table*
_____*Posture straight, body centered, eyes on screen*

Keyboarding Skills

_____*Reviewed mouse skills*
_____*Kept keyboard one inch off edge of table*
_____*Curled hands over keyboard, pointers on f and j*
_____*Used proper log-on/log-off procedures*
_____*Demonstrated proper care and handling of keyboard, mouse*
_____*Know location of important keys*
_____*Used right thumb to spacebar*
_____*Practiced keyboarding*
_____*Used school software and online sites for keyboarding*
_____*Practiced finger exercises*
_____*Learned useful shortkeys (i.e., Ctrl+S, Ctrl+C)*
_____*Memorized all keys*
_____*Keyboarded with hands covered*
_____*Used proper keyboarding skills every time you sat at computer*
_____*Evaluated handwriting vs. keyboarding speed*
_____*Participated in Annual Team Challenge—Keyboarding*

Problem-solving Skills

_____*Comfortable with 22 problems presented in this ebook*

Digital Citizenship

_____*Understand the parts of a website*
_____*Understand how to follow proper digital rights and responsibilities*
_____*Practiced good digital citizenship skills*
_____*Did not give out personal information—ever*
_____*Avoided ads*

Completed required projects:

_____ ***If using online video keyboarding course, you watched all required videos and completed all exercises***

_____ *Used websites to practice keyboarding skills*

_____ *Improved keyboarding speed and accuracy over the year*

_____ *Took 3 blank keyboard assessments to review your knowledge of key placement. Score improved from beginning of year to end.*

_____ *Use keyboarding to complete projects*

_____ *Finished monthly homework*

Thanks for purchasing!

Terms of Use
according to American Copyright Laws

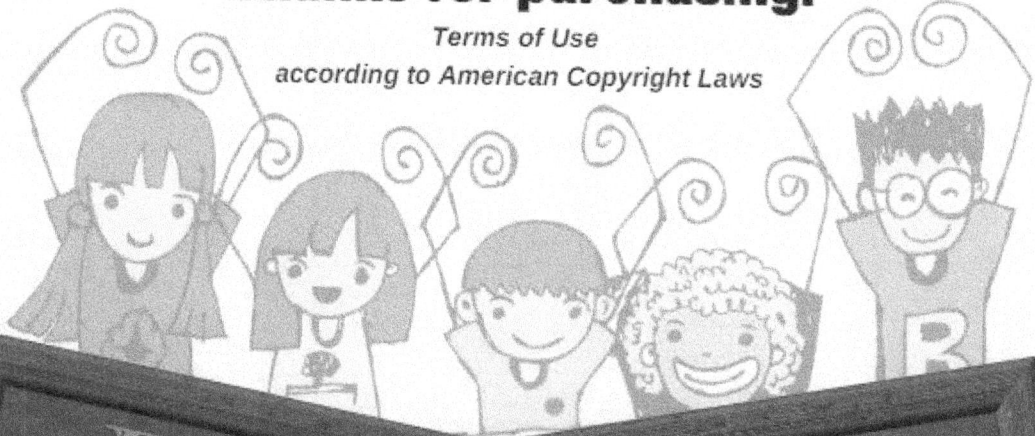

DO...

- Use this item for personal use, your class, your students
- Review/share your experiences online provided you link back to the AATT store
- Buy additional licenses

DON'T...

- Copy, email, or post to a shared account
- Post this item or a portion (> 10%) be it to your website, school server, another
- Share it, sell, claim it as your own
- Use any part of this to create another product for sharing, selling

Please visit me!